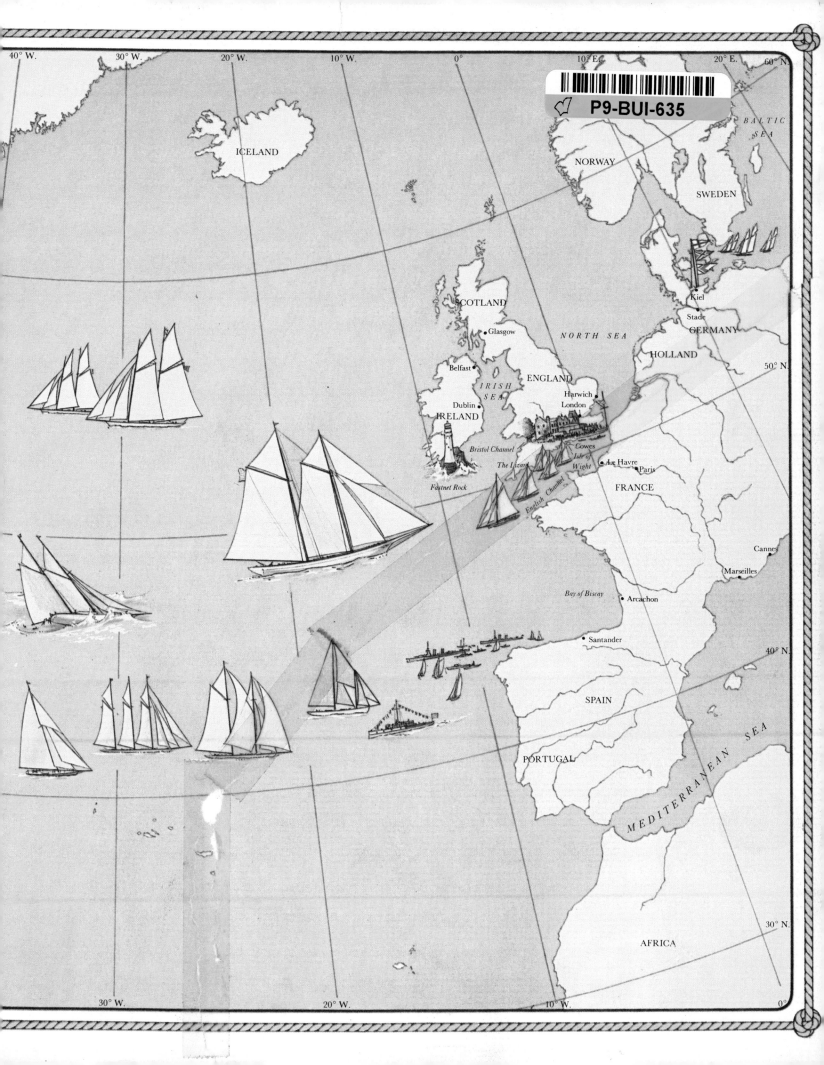

damaged
11-7-91

The Seafarers THE RACING
YACHTS

The Cover: In the first America's Cup race, run in 1870, the American schooner *Magic (foreground)* sails to victory in New York Harbor as codefenders *Dauntless*, *Idler* and *America* follow close behind her, and British challenger *Cambria* trails at far left. *Magic's* triumph was effusively hailed by one journalist as "the greatest victory ever won by a yacht since the world was young."

Weighing eight pounds six ounces and standing 27 inches high, the America's Cup is the universal symbol of yachting supremacy. Captured from Britain by the yacht *America* in 1851, the baroque trophy bears inscriptions that chronicle more than a century of repeated victories by American yachts over British, Australian and Canadian challengers.

The Seafarers

THE RACING YACHTS

by A. B. C. Whipple
AND THE EDITORS OF TIME-LIFE BOOKS

TIME-LIFE BOOKS, ALEXANDRIA, VIRGINIA

The Seafarers

Editorial Staff for *The Racing Yachts:*
Editor: Jim Hicks
Designer: Herbert H. Quarmby
Chief Researcher: W. Mark Hamilton
Picture Editor: John Conrad Weiser
Text Editors: Anne Horan, Stuart Gannes, Gus Hedberg.
Lydia Preston, Mark M. Steele, David Thiemann
Staff Writers: Kathleen M. Burke.
Donald Davison Cantlay
Researchers: Barbara Brownell, Mindy A. Daniels.
Philip Brandt George, Lois Gilman, Fran Glennon.
Sheila M. Green, Ann Dusel Kuhns
Art Assistant: Michelle René Clay
Editorial Assistant: Ellen Keir

Special Contributors
Bryce Walker (essays); Martha Reichard George
(research)

Editorial Production
Production Editor: Douglas B. Graham
Operations Manager: Gennaro C. Esposito.
Gordon E. Buck (assistant)
Assistant Production Editor: Feliciano Madrid
Quality Control: Robert L. Young (director). James J. Cox
(assistant). Daniel J. McSweeney. Michael G. Wight
(associates)
Art Coordinator: Anne B. Landry
Copy Staff: Susan B. Galloway (chief). Anne T. Connell.
Sheirazada Hann. Celia Beattie
Picture Department: Jane Martin
Traffic: Jeanne Potter

Correspondents: Elisabeth Kraemer (Bonn); Margot
Hapgood. Dorothy Bacon. Lesley Coleman (London);
Susan Jonas. Lucy T. Voulgaris (New York); Maria
Vincenza Aloisi, Josephine du Brusle (Paris); Ann
Natanson (Rome).
Valuable assistance was also provided by: Enid Farmer
(Boston); Connie Singer (Chicago); Ian Donaldson
(Halifax); Peter Collis (Lisbon); Karin B. Pearce (London);
Jane Walker. Trini Debelius (Madrid); Carolyn T. Chubet.
Miriam Hsia, Christina Lieberman (New York); Warren
Vieth (Oklahoma City); Susan Dowd (Philadelphia);
Mimi Murphy (Rome); Waverly Lowell. Janet Zich (San
Francisco); Mary Johnson (Stockholm); Stephen Marshall
(Wilmington).

The Author:
A.B.C. Whipple is an avid day sailor and
occasional offshore racer. A former assistant managing editor of Time-Life Books,
he is the author of many books about ships
and the sea, including *The Whalers, Fighting Sail* and *The Clipper Ships* in the Seafarers series.

The Consultants:
John Horace Parry, Gardiner Professor of
Oceanic History and Affairs at Harvard
University, is the author of such illustrious
historical studies as *The Discovery of the
Sea, Trade and Dominion* and *The Span-
ish Seaborne Empire.* He served in the
Royal Navy during World War II, rising to
the rank of commander.

Halsey Herreshoff is a naval architect and
a sailor of more than 30 years' experience.
He has served as navigator during several
defenses of the America's Cup and is a veteran of many ocean races, including the
Fastnet and Bermuda contests. His grand-
father, Nathanael Herreshoff *(pages 114-
115),* designed five Cup defenders, including the famed *Columbia* and *Reliance.*

John Rousmaniere has logged more than
15,000 miles of ocean racing, including
four races to Bermuda, one transatlantic
race and one Fastnet. He has written three
books on sailing and holds a master's degree in history from Columbia University.

Peter Snowden, veteran of practically every major European small-boat competition, managed the British racing team for
the Olympic Games sailing events at Na-
ples in 1960. He holds memberships in
several British yacht clubs, including the
Royal Yacht Squadron.

William Avery Baker, curator of the Hart
Nautical Museum at the Massachusetts Institute of Technology, is by training a naval architect and engineer. He has supervised construction of ships ranging from
reproductions of 17th and 18th Century
sailing vessels to supertankers.

For information about any Time-Life book. please write:
Reader Information. Time-Life Books.
541 North Fairbanks Court. Chicago. Illinois 60611.

TIME-LIFE is a trademark of Time Incorporated U.S.A.

Library of Congress Cataloguing in Publication Data
Whipple. Addison Beecher Colvin. 1918-
  Racing yachts.
  (The Seafarers)
  Bibliography: p.
  Includes index.
  1. Yacht racing—History.   I. Time-Life Books.
  II. Title.   III. Series: Seafarers.
GV826.5.W47   797.1'4   80-20463
ISBN 0-8094-2694-3
ISBN 0-8094-2695-1 (Regular bdg. : on subscription)
ISBN 0-8094-2694-3 (lib. bdg.)

Contents

Exhilarating tests of man and sail

"Yachting may be termed the poetry of the sea," wrote Arthur Clark, a 19th Century ship's captain. Although he sailed for a living, Clark was also a member of the New York Yacht Club who never missed a chance to take a yacht's helm for pleasure. "No other sport or pastime has been so interwoven with romance and countless memories of daring deeds and glorious achievements."

The lure of this dazzling sport, like poetry itself, eludes exact analysis. But it is compounded of the thrills attendant upon high speed and lurking danger, the insistent desire to outwit both sea and fellow yachtsmen, and the relentless demands for split-second calculations and rapid action—with helmsman, crew and yacht in perfect tune.

Perhaps the keenest exhilaration is reserved for the helmsman, who with the wheel in his hand feels "the trembling nerves of the great vessel vibrate," one skipper recalled, "so that the yacht becomes a living creature." But thrills for the spectator are hardly lacking—as is testified by the enthusiasts who crowd regattas all over the world. Reporting the 1851 race that eventually led to the establishment of the America's Cup series, *The Times of London* noted: "Steamers, shoreboats and yachts of all sizes buzzed along each side of the course and spread for miles over the rippling sea—a sight such as the Adriatic never beheld in all the pride of Venice."

This kind of enthusiasm, far from waning with other Victorian fancies, has mounted in the decades that have passed since then—and nowhere more so than in the waters off Cowes, the Isle of Wight village where the yacht-racing world's preeminent regatta has been staged every summer since 1826. In the course of Cowes Week in August 1975, more than 4,000 racers representing 19 nations competed in 650 yachts. As can be seen in the photographs on these pages, the clashes of big boats epitomize the spellbinding excitement that has made the era of yacht racing the last great age of sail.

Flying every sail in her locker, the American cutter Sonya surges into the lead in the downwind leg of a race off Cowes in 1911.

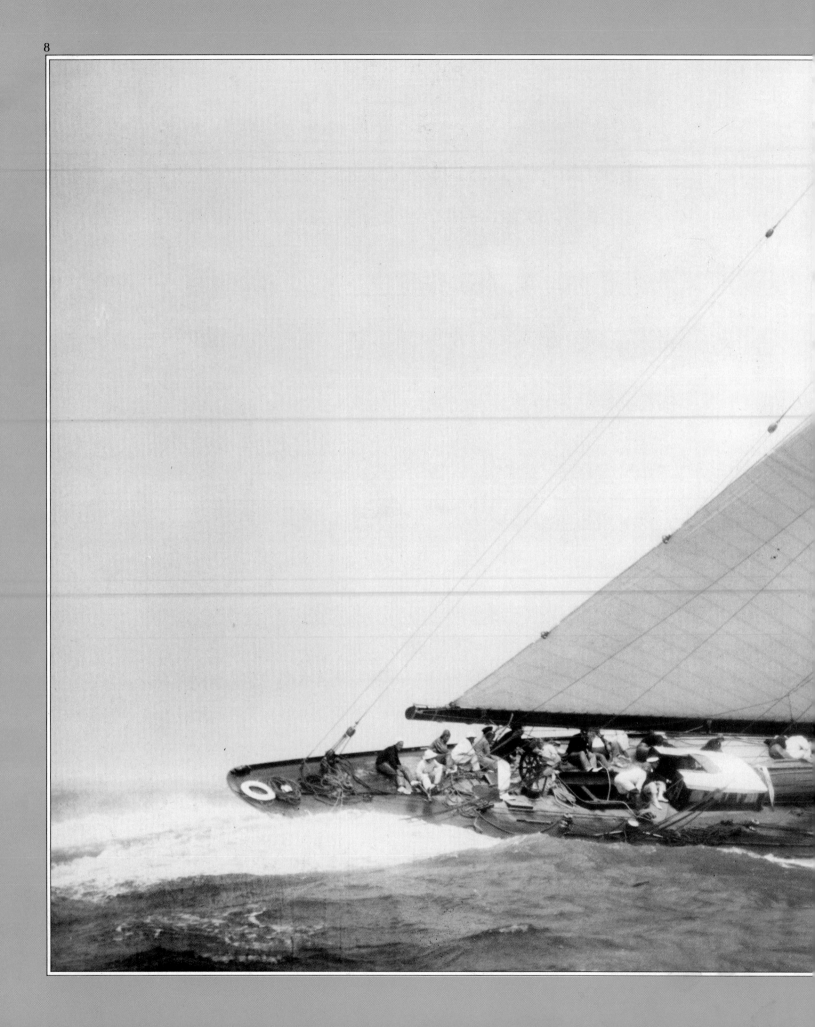

Bent on victory, Shamrock V—at 120 feet one of the largest racing yachts ever built—drives upwind in a heavy sea off the Isle of Wight in 1934.

With the lee rail awash, Candida's helmsman wrestles with her wheel to battle to windward during a British Royal Yacht Squadron race in 1930.

A foredeck hand aboard Candida raises his arm to signal victory to the crew as the yacht rips over the finish line in a 1934 race.

Chapter 1

A leisurely start for a sport of speed

On the first day of October 1661, a procession of vessels moved grandly, if somewhat haltingly, down the Thames River from Greenwich toward Gravesend, fighting an oncoming wind. Two royal yachts dominated the fleet, their bulwarks gleaming with gilded carvings, their huge banners whipping above their square topsails in the brisk breeze. King Charles II himself strode the deck of his yacht *Catherine*, and his brother James, Duke of York, was aboard his own new yacht, *Anne*. The King's barge, his kitchen boat and a retinue of other craft rowed by Royal Navy sailors danced attendance, oars flashing in the sunlight.

Gentlemen of Charles's glittering Restoration court, clad in knee breeches and bright, long-waisted coats, lounged about the decks of both royal yachts, gossiping, playing cards and watching the sailors at their work, while servants tendered goblets of wine and great silver platters of food. On either of the yachts, courtiers who sought respite from the activity on deck could descend an intricately carved staircase to an ornate great cabin. And if the royal brothers tired, they were able to find comfort and relaxation in their spacious, paneled staterooms, which were furnished with four-poster beds.

To most of those aboard the yachts, the occasion was a magnificent floating party; to anyone watching from shore, it appeared a fabulous royal pageant. Posterity, however, was to cherish the event as something else altogether: history's first formally organized yacht race. For, unlikely as it might seem, *Catherine* and *Anne* were engaged in a contest of speed. Moving so slowly that the attending vessels powered by oars had little trouble keeping up with them, the two royal yachts were racing nearly 40 miles from Greenwich to Gravesend and back, and a £100 wager between the King and his brother rode on the outcome. Other men had raced boats for pleasure before, of course, and almost certainly some had raced yachts. But this was the earliest contest to be recorded, and racing yachtsmen who are historically inclined view it as the birth of their sport, the precursor of more than three hundred years of glorious competition in which sailors have extended themselves and their vessels to the limits of their abilities for the pure exhilaration of the race and the thrill of winning.

For all Charles II's renown as a dilettante, the King was a physically tough man, a suitable father for the vigorous sport of yacht racing. He played a hard tennis match every day at 6 a.m., rode his own horses in the races at Newmarket and swam frequently in the Thames. Charles's passion for sailing was born during the English Civil War, when he

Flying the royal standard from her masthead, the yacht Mary, given to King Charles II of England by a Dutch admirer in 1660, beats up the Thames past the City of London. Charles was so smitten with yachting that he encouraged his nobles to take up the sport. He eventually commissioned some 30 swift pleasure craft as successors to Mary.

escaped aboard a frigate from Oliver Cromwell's vengeful Roundheads, and it was nurtured during 14 years of exile, spent largely among the seafaring people of the Netherlands.

In May 1660, during the first leg of his triumphal return to England after the death of Cromwell, Charles had been so captivated by his borrowed fleet of small Dutch vessels, called *jachts*, that the Dutch East India Company presented him with one, the 100-ton *Mary*—"one of the finest things that ever I saw for neatness and room in so small a vessel," wrote diarist Samuel Pepys. The King was so pleased with his new toy, Pepys noted, that he sometimes rose at 5 in the morning to visit the yacht, dragging his sleepy courtiers along with him. His enthusiasm for the vessel was such that he and James ordered the Admiralty to build two more boats, one for each of them.

Charles and James carried on a friendly sibling rivalry, characterized chiefly by sober James's inability to appreciate his brother's barbed wit: On one occasion when James chided the King for disregarding personal security, Charles reassured him: "I am sure no man in England will take away my life to make you King." It was in this same bantering spirit that Charles, on acquiring his new *Catherine* (named for his bride-to-be, Catherine of Braganza) in 1661, arranged a race against James's *Anne*.

While the royal yachts were utterly unlike the sleek racing machines of modern times, they were not as frivolous as their lavish appointments and decorations made them appear. A 17th Century yacht represented the apex of contemporary nautical architecture: a relatively fast seagoing vessel, originally designed for wartime use as an advice boat and scout, which was capable of carrying eight brass cannon and a crew of 30 navy tars. *Catherine* and *Anne* were perfect examples of the type, sister ships in nearly every respect.

Both boats were patterned after the Dutch *Mary*—*Catherine* by famous shipwright Christopher Pett, *Anne* by his brother Peter. The two yachts had virtually the same dimensions: The 94-ton *Catherine* measured about 55 feet overall and 19 feet at the beam, drawing seven feet of water; the 100-ton *Anne* was a trifle longer but otherwise identical. And they carried the same single-masted rigs, with twin headsails, a gaff mainsail and a square topsail towering above all. They were well matched for a trial of speed.

Forced to beat into a stiff easterly wind on the first leg of the race, the yachts laboriously worked their way back and forth across the half-mile-wide river like two ponderous crabs. Because neither vessel could point up well—that is, sail close to the wind—the wind caught their towering hulls almost broadside, pushing them nearly as far sideways as forward. As the two boats wallowed downstream like two floating barns, the Duke's yacht proved that she could point up a bit better. The King lost the first leg of the race.

From the only surviving account of the contest—an entry in the diary of John Evelyn, a man of letters and court gadabout who was aboard *Catherine*—it seems that Charles and James agreed to start afresh for the homeward leg of the race, rather than simply to round a mark at Gravesend. And, as often happens, the boat that sailed badly while beating

A crowd of some 50,000 spectators gathers to cheer Charles II, newly restored as the English monarch, upon the departure of his fleet from Scheveningen, Holland, on May 23, 1660. During the two-day passage to England, the King dined in regal splendor aboard the elegantly appointed ship Royal Charles. His penchant for cruising in style would later be indulged with even more lavishness aboard his yachts.

against the wind did better when running before it. The King himself occasionally took the helm as *Catherine* surged forward, her shivering canvas goosewinged—headsails ballooning over the starboard bow and mainsail boomed out to port—her long pennant snapping ahead in the breeze. *Catherine* apparently swept past Greenwich ahead of *Anne*, ending the race in a draw at one leg each. The King, as Evelyn reported, "saved stakes" on his wager.

Through the centuries since that royal contest, racing under sail for pleasure has become a much more demanding enterprise—and a much more democratic one, although until relatively recent times it continued to be primarily a rich man's sport that numbered kings and princes among its most avid participants. But even wealthy racing yachtsmen had to be willing to take the same punishment that the sea meted out to those who sailed for a living, and all for the satisfaction of proving their own skills and their yachts' speed and endurance. Many a merchant skipper, in foul weather off England's Solent or New Jersey's Sandy Hook, has shaken his head at the sight of a fleet of racing yachts pounding through heavy seas and has wondered what kind of fools would venture out in such conditions for pleasure.

In their bravery, competitiveness and resourcefulness, racing yachtsmen have provided dramatic epics of adventurous seamanship, and—

all in the name of sport—they have pushed the development of fast sailing vessels far beyond the levels of refinement achieved over thousands of years by working mariners.

The sharp challenge of racing, in fact, led the English to begin improving the yacht almost as soon as they got their hands on it. Dutch yachts, in order to sail in Holland's shallow waters, depended on leeboards, rather than keels, to keep from being swept sideways by the wind: A board was slung along each side, and the leeward one was dropped into the water to counteract drifting. Since British waters were generally deeper than those of the Netherlands, English shipbuilders soon began fitting their yachts with deep keels, which were much more effective than leeboards; Charles's and James's British-made yachts had such keels. The King's shipwrights also constantly tinkered with the ballasting of the royal yachts. When the Naval Commissioners suggested economizing on one of Charles's yachts by using stone ballast rather than 16 tons of expensive lead musket shot, her builder, Christopher Pett, indignantly replied that "the King's new yacht will be damaged, for the quantity of stones required would make it needful to half fill the cabin, and would make her run to leeward."

King Charles himself did not hesitate to intervene in such matters. He was so disappointed with *Catherine*'s initial performance that he ordered a whole new suit of sails less than two months after her launch, specifying an expensive Dutch cotton duck instead of baggy, porous French canvas. And Charles claimed credit for inventing the ketch, a two-masted vessel. His first ketch, a yacht named *Fubbs*, had square sails on the mainmast and a lateen sail on the mizzen. While there were earlier vessels with two masts, the King's example did in fact do much to popularize the ketch.

Making ample use of his royal prerogative, Charles owned and sailed nearly 30 yachts during his 25-year reign. The King's enthusiasm soon infected his nobles, whose commissions so overwhelmed shipwright Christopher Pett that he applied for permission to levy a special surcharge on yachts to pay for the food and drink consumed by noble visitors to his shipyard. When these novice mariners set sail, they often fell victim to the bane of yachtsmen, seasickness. When Sir William Batten, one of the first private yachtsmen, took his wife out on a windy September cruise in 1663, Samuel Pepys noted in his diary that "they will be sick enough, as my lady is mighty troublesome on the water"— and later observed that Lady Batten "has been so sick she swears never to go to sea again." The King, who could handle a helm and reef a sail as well as a seaman could, prided himself on never being queasy at sea and had little sympathy for such sufferers.

Charles's love of the sea never flagged. Samuel Pepys wrote that the King "possessed a transcendant mastery of all maritime knowledge, and two leagues travel at sea was more pleasure to him than twenty by land." He often spent his leisure time aboard a yacht that was permanently moored alongside his Whitehall palace. But the popular enthusiasm of the early 1660s quickly waned. After London suffered through the plague in 1665 and the Great Fire of 1666, the city was

King Charles II, a fervent champion of the naval sciences, points out some of the navigator's paraphernalia that intrigued him: a telescope; an armillary sphere, used to study the movements of heavenly bodies; a globe of the world; and (right foreground) a cross-staff, for measuring the elevation of the sun or stars.

without the economic resources to support such a frivolous pastime. When Charles II died in 1685, his fleet of yachts was transferred to the Royal Navy, and yacht racing seemed to die with him; his successors on the throne demonstrated much less interest in the sport. Moreover, several decades of intermittent naval skirmishes against the Dutch and other foreign powers made yacht cruising outside the Thames estuary a perilous recreation.

The hiatus lasted for nearly a century. The writer Samuel Johnson reflected the opinion of the age when he remarked: "He who goes to sea for pleasure would go to Hell for a pastime." When racing was again taken up, it happened almost by accident. On June 4, 1749, the 11-year-old Prince of Wales, later to be King George III, awarded a silver cup to the winner of a rowing contest on the Thames. Afterward, someone suggested that in fairness he ought to offer a matching prize for a sailing race. Prince George immediately acquiesced, sponsoring a 12-boat race from Greenwich to The Nore, a sandbank about 40 miles distant at the mouth of the Thames, and back.

The race lasted all day, all night and part of the next afternoon. The yacht *Princess Augusta*, owned by a man named George Bellas, took command from the start, and had left the rest of the fleet a mile astern by the time she reached Woolwich, about five miles downstream. She was three miles ahead before she reached The Nore. On the return leg Prin-

King Charles II's courtly custom of naming his yachts after his mistresses began in 1671 with the christening of Cleveland (foreground) in honor of Barbara Villiers, Duchess of Cleveland (inset). In this portrait she holds the future Duke of Southampton, first of five children she bore Charles during the early years of his restoration to the throne.

Charles's yacht Portsmouth, named by
the King as a compliment to his
paramour Louise de Kéroualle, Duchess
of Portsmouth (inset), rides at anchor
in this contemporary painting. Louise was
also the inspiration for the name of
the yacht Fubbs—a nickname meaning
"chubby" that the King jestingly
applied to the elegant French courtesan.

cess Augusta slipped to third place at Gravesend, but she recovered the
lead and won by 10 minutes.

The festive scene at the finish line on that sunny summer afternoon
was testimony to the sudden renewal of the sport's popularity: The
Gentleman's Magazine reported that "the river seemed overspread with
sailing yachts, galleys, and small boats." Prince George and his attendants greeted the victors from what a witness described as "a Chinese
barge" with "rowers in Chinese habits," and led the yachts in a triumphant procession up the Thames, the young Prince doffing his hat to
frequent huzzahs from the yachtsmen.

George III was not a racing yachtsman himself, preferring naval reviews and sedate cruises. But the woman he married proved herself, on
at least one occasion, a truly intrepid sailor. She was a German princess,
Charlotte of Mecklenburg-Strelitz. In 1761, after Charlotte's betrothal to
George, the ship-rigged, 232-ton yacht Royal Caroline was renamed
Royal Charlotte in her honor and was dispatched to convey her to England. Since the royal wedding and the coronation already had been
scheduled, the Charlotte, escorted by a fleet of men-of-war and three
other royal yachts, was forced to set sail from Stade despite a raging
North Sea tempest. During the voyage the fleet encountered three
successive storms, once sighting the English coast only to be driven back
almost to Norway. The Royal Charlotte took 10 days to sail the roughly

400 miles to Harwich. Princess Charlotte, far from being seasick, seemed to enjoy the awesome onslaught of the waves, bracing herself in the pitching cabin and comforting her queasy, terrified retinue with gay tunes on the harpsichord.

The renaissance of yacht racing during King George's 60-year reign was fostered largely by his brother Henry Frederick, the Duke of Cumberland. A Royal Navy admiral and ardent sailor, the Duke frequently cruised the Thames with an informal group of yachtsmen. On July 6, 1775, the Duke placed a notice in the London *Public Advertiser*: "A silver cup, the gift of His Royal Highness the Duke of Cumberland, is to be sailed for on Tuesday, the 11th instant, from Westminster Bridge to Putney Bridge and back, by Pleasure Sailing Boats, from two to five tons burthen." Entries were confined to "those boats which were never let out to hire." And the newspapers soon reported a note that has echoed down the centuries to the present: "The Gentlemen, about 18 or 20 in number, who sail for the prize have come to a resolution to be dressed in aquatic uniforms." Yachtsmen have continued to dress up in some form of nautical uniform for special occasions ever since.

Postponed once because of unsuitable weather, the race finally was run on July 13. Unlike the cruising yachts in earlier races, the vessels in this contest were designed primarily for speed, being patterned after the revenue cutters used for chasing smugglers. A fleet of some 20 small boats—single-masted, barely 20 feet long and seven feet broad, with

A twin-hulled vessel three centuries before its time

"We are surely fallen upon a new and better principle of shipping," wrote English inventor Sir William Petty in 1662. Sailing men still debate whether his idea was better, but Petty was certainly correct in saying it was new: His creation was nothing less than the Western world's first catamaran.

Petty, a physician, anatomist and dilettante in other sciences, postulated that a slim cylindrical hull would slice the water like an arrow, and that two cylinders bridged by a deck would form so stable a vessel that "there will bee noe danger of oversetting."

His first "fantastical double-bottom machine," as King Charles II described it, was launched in 1662 and dubbed *Invention*. It was a crude platform secured to two cylinders, each two feet in diameter and 20 feet long, and fitted with a single sail. Although primitive, *Invention* was fast, beating three conventional sailboats in a race along the Irish coast. A more streamlined *Invention II*, completed in 1663, proved even faster, besting one of the King's swift packets in a race on Dublin Bay.

Petty's third catamaran, *Experiment* (right), foundered in a Bay of Biscay gale during a 1665 voyage intended to demonstrate her seaworthiness. This disaster caused him to give up his experiments until 1684, when, struck again by "fits of the Double Bottom," he launched *St. Michael*. She proved unstable and was scrapped after a trial sail. Petty died three years later.

Mariners have shown little interest in his innovation. It was not until the 20th Century, when multihulled yachts finally won worldwide popularity, that Petty's vision was at last brought to full fruition.

William Petty: anatomist and builder of catamarans

sharp, deep keels—anchored in line for the start, sails furled. At the gun, each of the three-man crews frantically weighed anchor, hoisted the gaff mainsail and single jib, and surged ahead on the 12-mile course. After the race, the winner, a Mr. Parkes of Ludgate Hill, went ashore to receive the Duke's 20-guinea cup in a ceremony that was repeated annually in succeeding years: The Duke filled the cup with claret and drank Mr. Parkes's health. Mr. Parkes in turn quaffed the cup, toasting the health of the Duke and Duchess, to great cheers and salvos of cannon.

The Duke's patronage provided the impetus for the founding of England's first yacht club, the Cumberland Fleet, which was formed soon after the race. (Only one sailing organization is known to have predated the Cumberland Fleet. In 1720 a somewhat bibulous band of Irishmen had formed the Water Club of the Harbour of Cork, a social fraternity that occasionally staged waterborne reviews and mock battles, but apparently never raced.) In its early days the Fleet devoted most of its time to staging elaborate nautical pageants and reviews, but each year it also organized two or three serious races on the Thames, including a race for the Duke's cup (he donated a new one every year).

When the Duke's interest waned in the mid-1780s, his place as London's leading patron of yachting was taken by Jonathon Tyars, the proprietor of Vauxhall Gardens, a fashionable London amusement park on the banks of the Thames. Tyars' annual Vauxhall Cup race became a glamorous spectacle rivaling the other attractions of Vauxhall Gardens,

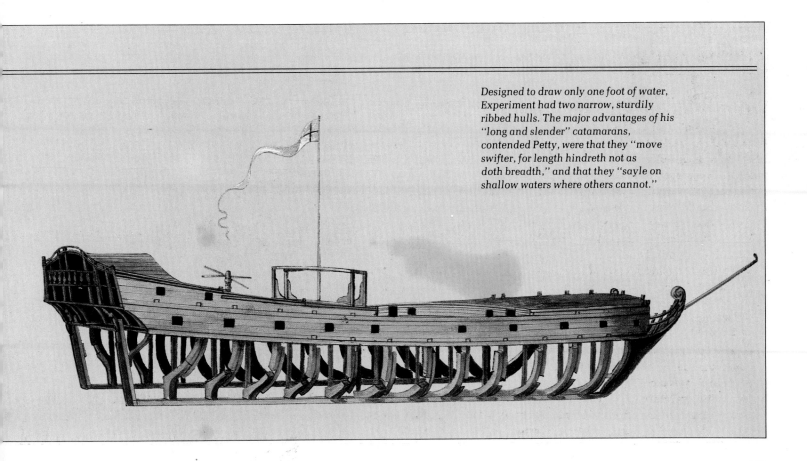

Designed to draw only one foot of water, Experiment had two narrow, sturdily ribbed hulls. The major advantages of his "long and slender" catamarans, contended Petty, were that they "move swifter, for length hindreth not as doth breadth," and that they "sayle on shallow waters where others cannot."

such as dances, concerts and banquets. The enterprising Tyars fitted out a barge as Neptune's chariot, drawn by Tritons and carrying costumed river gods (including Father Thames) and bands of musicians. Such imaginative gimmicks—and the growing popularity of yacht racing itself—attracted enormous crowds of spectators. "The river was so completely covered with boats," said a contemporary account of one race, "that it reminded one of the descriptions given of the swarm of canoes that assembled upon Captain Cook making his appearance in New South Wales." Another report claimed that "the Thames could be walked across at some places by stepping from boat to boat."

Before the races the captains of the Cumberland Fleet would meet convivially at the Crown and Anchor, a tavern on the Strand, to draw lots for starting positions. But once on water, the contest resembled naval combat as much as a trial of speed. Lacking a formal code of racing rules, captains frequently would attempt to "ride out" another boat more in the manner of polo than yachting. When rigging and bowsprits became hopelessly tangled, crews slashed each other's ropes with cutlasses. On at least one occasion a yacht limped home under jury rig after an opposing captain all but dismasted her; in another race, reported the London *Morning Chronicle*, a yacht that had been rammed "got all clear by a liberal use of handspikes."

The royal yacht Charlotte (center), festooned with flags and flanked by an escort of warships and smaller yachts, sets out from Stade, Germany, in 1761 to convey her namesake, Princess Charlotte of Mecklenburg-Strelitz, across the English Channel to wed King George III. The 232-ton Charlotte sailed for 54 years, from 1749 until 1803.

Although the Cumberland Fleet commanded the allegiance of many middle-class yachtsmen, the rich, aristocratic elite of the sport sneered at the Fleet's modest boats, some as small as four tons. These blue-blooded yachtsmen, who sailed large seagoing vessels ranging up to more than 100 tons, naturally gravitated to England's finest yachting grounds—the waters off the Isle of Wight, five miles southwest of Portsmouth. The island itself, a fashionable summer resort since Roman times, in the early 19th Century became a favorite rendezvous for yachtsmen, in part because it could be reached only by boat. They gathered annually at Cowes, a resort village on the island's northern shore, for sailing and festive dinners.

This genteel tradition soon gave birth to a formal organization. On June 1, 1815, some 30 of these yachtsmen met at the Thatched House Tavern on St. James's Street, London, to form what they called simply—and somewhat haughtily, considering the prior existence of the Cumberland Fleet—the Yacht Club. The sole qualification for membership was ownership of a yacht of not less than 10 tons; but to further ensure the club's exclusivity, the 42 founding members—among them two marquesses, three earls, four viscounts, four barons and five baronets—provided that two blackballs could bar an applicant. This expedient restricted membership more effectively than anyone could have imagined, largely because of the whimsy of the members. One irascible yachtsman simply blackballed a candidate whenever the wind was in the east. According to a member, a candidate needed three qualities to escape blackballing: "He must be adequately well born. He must be a good companion. He must be able to get tight without becoming disagreeable, or he must get tight and go to sleep."

The snobbery of the Yacht Club was so pervasive that the founders felt self-obliged to pass a resolution that waived social protocol in the event of a maritime emergency: "Although many members of this club are not personally acquainted, it is hoped that no introduction will be deemed necessary in any case where assistance by boats or otherwise may be required."

The club's punctilious regulations tightened further when the Prince Regent—Prince George, a dissolute, universally detested ruler but a yachtsman—joined the club in 1817. To preserve the proper standards, the minimum yacht size was raised to 20 tons and later to 30 tons, and soon the club adopted an official uniform, a blue jacket with white trousers—"and to such as are not too square in the stern," reported the club's minutes, "it is far from being an unbecoming dress." When the Prince Regent became King George IV in 1820, he granted the club's eager petition to change its name to the Royal Yacht Club. At that time, scarcely a hundred men in Britain owned yachts large enough to qualify for membership in the exclusive club, and by 1823 only 71 of these had actually managed to make the roster.

Characteristically, the hidebound club bitterly resisted the advent of steam yachts—although members happily made use of the convenient packet service between the Isle of Wight and Southampton. In 1825, a Southampton newspaper complained that the clouds of coal-black smoke from these ferries "completely obscured all distant objects. The

Idylls of sail on landlocked royal waters

While King Charles II was racing yachts on the Thames, his cousin King Louis XIV of France also took up boating—but in a manner at once more grandiose and less adventurous. In the midst of Versailles's manicured gardens he created his own Grand Canal, an enclosed, placid stretch of water where his court could take part in boating festivals with no danger and with little chance of even getting wet.

The idea for this waterway that went nowhere originated with Louis's Secretary of State for the Navy, Jean Baptiste Colbert, who sold the King on building the mile-long, rectangular pool for testing scaled-down warships. But by the time it was completed in 1680, after 12 years of work and an outlay of more than one million livres, pleasure boating had replaced naval experimentation as the King's passion.

Although his built-to-scale Versailles fleet did include a couple of frigates and a 32-gun battleship, Louis preferred to cruise the pool in two English yachts, designed by the eminent naval architect Anthony Deane. He also prized his flotilla of graceful gondolas, which allowed him to re-create the aura of elegant Venice. The gondolas came with a retinue of Italian gondoliers, and these men, along with a staff of some 60 soldiers, naval carpenters and calkers who looked after the other craft, were housed in a hamlet known as Little Venice, on the grounds adjacent to the canal.

When marshaled for Louis's exquisite pageants, all his richly gilded vessels were decorated with crimson ropes and flew lustrous damask streamers from their masts. Throughout the Versailles summers, the King and his courtiers dallied until late at night in gala rounds of cruises, mock battles, fireworks displays and shipboard feasts.

Not to be outdone by his cousin, King Charles ordered the construction of his own artificial sailor's paradise in London's St. James's Park. There a series of swamps and ponds was converted into the King's Canal, where Charles spent many an afternoon racing in expressly designed small yachts. Although the entertainments in St. James's Park equaled the Versailles fetes in magnificence, Charles's concourse was also the scene of more egalitarian festivities. In the winter, the canal served as a skating rink, where the King's common subjects enjoyed spins on the ice.

Gondolas, yachts and other craft float alongside a scaled-down three-masted battleship on Louis XIV's Grand Canal at Versailles.

murky vomitings of the furnaces covered the surface of Southampton Water from side to side."

Four years later, the club adopted a resolution calling for the ejection of any member "applying a steam engine to his yacht." In part, this rule was directed specifically at Thomas Assheton-Smith, a prominent founding member who was the owner of five sailing yachts and who already had decided to commission a £20,000 steam yacht. Some of the club members darkly hinted that Assheton-Smith planned to make use of his steam yacht in trade. Assheton-Smith was "naturally enough very indignant at so unjust an accusation," one of his friends later wrote, and he immediately withdrew from the club. As late as 1843, the club adopted a half-humorous resolution proposing that steamers that belonged to members be required to "consume their own smoke," which effectively barred owners of steam yachts from membership. They finally gained admission a year later.

For all the club's hauteur, it boasted a salty, hardy cadre of yachtsmen whose eccentricities and exploits, both on and off the water, became the stuff of legend. The Marquess of Anglesey, for example, was sitting on his horse at the Battle of Waterloo, when a cannonball severed his leg. Looking down, Anglesey commented conversationally to the Duke of Wellington, who was next to him, "By God, I've lost my leg," whereupon the equally phlegmatic Wellington replied, "By God, so you have." The injury kept Anglesey from sailing his yacht *Pearl* that season, but he was back at her helm the following year, and he continued stumping around his quarter-deck for another 38 years. Lord Anglesey christened his son Alfred, shortly after his birth, by plunging him from the deck of *Pearl* headfirst into the sea. The marquess eventually was named Governor of the Isle of Wight, and when he died in 1858 the Yacht Club inherited his magnificent castle on the waterfront, originally constructed by Henry VIII, to use as its new headquarters. The castle's stubby tower, low battlements and sweeping lawn have been the cynosure of European yachting ever since.

One notable eccentric, the Marquess of Waterford—who was said to while away his evenings after the port and brandy by shooting out the eyes of his family portraits with his pistol—was a formidable racing yachtsman aboard his schooner *Gem*. He prided himself on his fearlessness. During one contest, when his cap blew overboard he chased it to the ship's rail, dived overboard after it and was swept away by the tide. He was finally rescued, half drowned; it is not known whether he managed to retrieve the cap.

Another high-spirited sailor, Lord Belfast, delighted in taunting the Royal Navy with his sleek brig *Waterwitch*. He often sailed idly back and forth outside Portsmouth harbor until some naval ships appeared, then proceeded to overtake them and ostentatiously shorten sail while maintaining or increasing his lead. The Admiralty eventually put an end to this embarrassment by buying *Waterwitch* in 1834, and for the next decade the Royal Navy's 10-gun brigs were built to her design.

Members did not confine their sailing to the waters around the Isle of Wight. They often voyaged to the annual summer rendezvous via the French ports of Cherbourg and Bordeaux, where they laid down sup-

plies—principally wine—for the festive Cowes dinners; some also ventured into the Baltic, the Mediterranean and the West Indies. The British Admiralty decreed that club yachts, which were empowered by special warrant to fly the white ensign of the Royal Navy, should in Mediterranean ports be accorded the same privileges and honors as British warships, and most European nations exempted them from port fees as well. One restless club sailor, a stockbroker named Benjamin Boyd, took his yacht *Wanderer* around Cape Horn to Australia, used her for whale hunting in the Antarctic, cruised to California to dig for gold and to the South Pacific to hunt game in the Solomon Islands—where he abruptly disappeared, purportedly a victim of cannibals.

At first, the club's yachts, like many before them, engaged primarily in sailing processions; but from the beginning few members could resist the challenge of a match race—and of a healthy wager. Rivals routinely bet as much as £500 on a race, and side bets by their partisans ran into thousands of pounds. When Lord Belfast in *Waterwitch* defeated C.R.M. Talbot's *Galatea* in a two-day, 224-mile race around Eddystone Lighthouse in 1834, £50,000 reportedly changed hands.

Although the club loosely supervised these matches, it did not actually sponsor races itself until 1826. In that year it organized a series of races and social events that were the genesis of what is known today as Cowes Week. The first race, on August 10, was around an elaborate 40-mile course with four marks, and the prize was a £100 gold cup. In order to reduce the chaos and collisions that ordinarily attended such contests, the club promulgated for the first time a right-of-way rule that has applied ever since: "Vessels on the larboard tack were to give way for those on the starboard, and any vessel running foul of another shall lose the race." The next day, August 11, began with a festive review of pilot boats "belonging to the Isle of Wight," which was followed by a race for boats of less than 40 tons, with prizes for everyone who competed, ranging from £30 for the winning yacht to £2 for each loser. After the races there was a round of parties that would become a Cowes Week institution, capped by the annual Regatta Ball and a splendid display of fireworks along the esplanade.

The club's new right-of-way rule managed to control some of the hooliganism that had enlivened earlier races, but it did not eliminate waterborne combat altogether. Most of the yachts at Cowes were considerable vessels of 200 tons or more that were built, manned and armed like small naval ships. Most yachts mounted at least 10 brass cannon, to be used both for signaling and to defend themselves against pirates and privateers on the high seas, and all carried racks of rifles and cutlasses. The club's first commodore, Lord Yarborough, employed a Royal Navy lieutenant as skipper of his 351-ton *Falcon* and required the 54 crewmen to sign articles that proclaimed strict naval discipline, including punishment by flogging for insubordination.

Some races were literally fought to a finish. During one hotly contested 1829 race, Joseph Weld's *Lulworth* and Lord Belfast's *Louisa* struggled back to Cowes only seconds apart in such light air that night fell while the contest was under way. As they approached the finish line, shrouded by darkness, *Lulworth*, on a port tack, crashed into *Louisa* amidships, locking the two vessels together. What happened next was like war at sea. The crew members began slashing at each other's rigging, while—quite coincidentally—the night sky erupted with fireworks and yachts anchored nearby fired salvos of cannon in celebration of the King's birthday, bathing the embattled yachts in an eerie, flickering light. Before the combatants finally separated, *Louisa's* crew cut away *Lulworth's* earing (the rope lashing the sail to the yard) and her reef pendant, disabling her mainsail.

Lord Belfast and Mr. Weld both stormed ashore to the clubhouse, furious not only because they had collided but because they had missed the club's dinner. Weld protested the race, blaming Belfast for the collision. The stewards awarded the race to Belfast because his yacht had been on the starboard tack, but it also threw a sop to Weld, ruling that "the use of axes by *Louisa's* crew in the cutting away of rigging was unjustifiable"—albeit only because axes (as opposed to cutlasses) were considered unsporting.

Thereafter, Belfast vowed that he would cut in two any yacht that violated his right of way, and he nearly made good on the threat in the course of the next race, running into Thomas Assheton-Smith's *Menai*. Belfast's offended adversaries withdrew en masse from the races scheduled for the remainder of the season, and the quarrel was not patched over until the following year.

When George IV died in 1830, his successor as King and as the club's royal patron was another yachting aficionado, King William IV. No amateur in nautical matters, William had served in the Royal Navy for some 10 years and now followed the club's affairs closely, particularly its races. He continued a tradition begun by George IV, each year presenting a £100 King's Cup during Cowes Week, while his sister-in-law, the Duchess of Kent, sponsored one of the challenge cups. And in 1833, at Lord Belfast's suggestion, he proclaimed the club, "as a mark of his Majesty's gracious approval of an institution of such national utility," the Royal Yacht Squadron, by which name it has been known ever since.

The following year William took steps to bring order to racing's chaos. The squadron had already experimented with a handicap system, dividing yachts into classes determined by their tonnage, and assigning each class a course of different length for the same race—a forerunner of the rating and time-allowance regulations that would bedevil future race committees. William saw an easier way. He simply decreed that "the King's Cup shall be sailed for by one class of the Royal Yacht Squadron each year," with the race rotating among eight classes.

The new policy caused consternation among the squadron's old-time yachtsmen, who had been accustomed to winning races simply by building bigger and bigger boats. "It was always intended," the *Sporting Magazine* correspondent wrote, "that the King's Cup should be a premium to the fastest vessel, but owing to the jealousies of the owners of the inferior classes of cutters, a wretched craft, not worth half the value of the Cup, by being the best of a bad lot may positively walk off with the

English gentlefolk stroll along the promenade at Cowes, the Isle of Wight resort adopted as headquarters by the Royal Yacht Squadron upon its establishment in 1815. When this sketch was made 10 years later, the club had nearly 100 members—including King George IV—and had attained a nationwide reputation for elegance.

gift of the Sovereign that was originally intended to promote the building of vessels of a superior class."

The advocates of the rule remained adamant, however, and carried the day. Contests for the King's Cup thereafter were sailed according to handicap rules that encouraged smaller boats, setting a trend that soon brought to an end the supremacy of the huge yachts.

William's successor, his 18-year-old niece Victoria, was already a summertime resident of the Isle of Wight and a frequent spectator at the squadron's yacht races when she ascended the throne in 1837. She continued royal patronage of the squadron and, by virtue of being Queen and sovereign, became during the first year of her reign its first woman member. In the heady Victorian era of gentlemen's clubs and outdoor sports, yachting thrived and proliferated in other places as well. Queen Victoria became a patroness of the Royal Thames Yacht Club (formerly the Cumberland Fleet) and, among others, the Royal London, Royal Gibraltar, Royal Eastern and Royal Southern Yacht Clubs (the latter two located at Edinburgh and Southampton, respectively). Beyond the boundaries of the British Empire, yacht clubs were founded in Sweden and, in 1844, in New York.

Although by midcentury American clipper ships were repeatedly humiliating their British competitors, the insular British yachtsmen still viewed the upstart Americans with a mixture of amusement and condescension, as if they were not civilized enough to enjoy a sophisticated sport like yachting. So it was with some astonishment that, early in 1851, the members of the Royal Yacht Squadron learned that a syndicate of New York Yacht Club members planned to build a yacht expressly to race the British in their home waters. The squadron's commodore, the Earl of Wilton, was too canny to blindly challenge the Americans to such a match. But he did send a cordial note to the commodore of the New York Yacht Club, John Cox Stevens:

"7, Grosvenor Square, London
"28th February, 1851

"Sir, Understanding from Sir H. Bulwer that a few of the members of the New York Yacht Club are building a schooner which it is their intention to bring over to England this summer, I have taken the liberty of writing to you in your capacity of Commodore, to request you to convey to them, and to any friends that may accompany them on board the yacht, an invitation on the part of myself and the members of the Royal Yacht Squadron to become visitors of the Clubhouse at Cowes during their stay in England.

"For myself, I may be permitted to say that I shall have great pleasure in extending to your countrymen any civility that lies in my power, and shall be very glad to avail myself of any improvements in shipbuilding that the industry and skill of your nation have enabled you to elaborate.

"I remain, Sir, Your obedient servant,
"Wilton
"Commodore R.Y.S."

The schooner to which Lord Wilton referred was named *America*. And before the year was out, his lordship would have good cause to regret having extended that invitation.

Chapter 2

"America": a hawk among the pigeons

Racing around in yachts was a novel idea to most Americans before the middle of the 19th Century. Few could afford to build large pleasure craft, and those who could were too busy compounding their fortunes to think of yachting. The young country, however, was very much a seafaring nation. American whalers were all over the Pacific, and American clipper ships were electrifying the maritime world by breaking speed records in every ocean. And as the country had few good roads, even most of the travel up and down the Eastern United States was by sea. In only three months of 1851, for example, more than 6,500 vessels passed Cuttyhunk Island, between New York and Boston.

There were, of course, a few boats built strictly for pleasure use in both of those big cities, and occasionally some engaged in impromptu races. A group of Boston yachtsmen went so far as to form a club—America's first yacht club—in 1834 (page 35), but it finally disbanded three years later. In 1845 the Boston suburb of Nahant staged a regatta for local runabouts and fishing craft. But organized yacht racing—that is, carefully monitored contests between vessels designed and built primarily for speed—really began in New York.

Historians have described the 1840s as America's awkward age, referring to the contrast between the young republic's booming prosperity and its social and cultural ungainliness. New York City was a sprawling giant of jumbled wood houses and gaudy neoclassical edifices, encircled by a dense hedge of ships' masts. It bustled with an air of self-importance and a heavy sense that the eyes of the rest of the world were upon it. In 1842, for instance, a fashionable New Yorker named Lydia Maria Child noted that "the number of servants in livery visibly increases every season and foreign artistic upholsterers assert that there will soon be more houses in New York furnished according to the taste and fashion of nobleness than there are even in Paris or London." That same year Charles Dickens, then making a tour through the New World, found New York on the whole "a beautiful metropolis," but was constrained to report that herds of pigs circulated freely about the streets, scavenging cabbage stalks and other garbage.

Since the city was both an island and a seaport, it was only natural that New York spawned what became America's oldest surviving yacht club. Many wealthy New Yorkers kept small sailing vessels for personal use, and the city's shipyards, which were famous for the swift transatlantic packets they produced, provided an abundance of top-notch shipwrights and designers. But it was an extraordinary group of brothers named Stevens who did more than any other New Yorkers to popularize the sport of yacht racing.

Their father, Colonel John Stevens, had fought in the Continental Army and had then settled on a large tract of land on the New Jersey side of the Hudson River, directly across from New York City. He made a fortune designing and building steamships and railways. His four sons emulated their father, proving to be ingenious inventors (pages 38-39) and building the already large family fortune into one of New York's largest. In 1838 Colonel Stevens died and his eldest son, John Cox Stevens, inherited the New Jersey estate, which included a hilltop mansion,

In a lithograph saluting American industrial accomplishments, displayed at London's Crystal Palace during the Great Exhibition of 1851, artist Charles Rodgers gives pride of place to the schooner America, which astonished the world that year with her victory over Britain's finest racing yachts.

called the Castle, that overlooked the Hudson. The new head of the family soon supplemented this residence with a large town house in New York's Washington Square.

In addition to managing his fortune and working on inventions, John Cox Stevens ran a steamship line. He also spent a great deal of time exercising his talents as a sportsman. He frequented New York's race tracks, wagering large sums he could well afford; he owned a famous race horse named Eclipse, and he was president of the Jockey Club for a number of years. He also introduced cricket to the United States, and when jingoistic Americans criticized him as an Anglophile, he installed a baseball diamond near his estate, in a park named Elysian Fields. But the sport that intrigued him earliest and eventually came to monopolize his time was yacht racing.

John Cox Stevens' first yacht was the 20-foot *Diver*, built for him in 1809 when he was 24 years old. Soon, like Charles II before him and so many yachtsmen to follow, he progressed to a bigger vessel, a 56-footer whose hull was styled after the pirogues of the Caribbean Indians. Because of problems in her construction, he christened her *Trouble*. By 1820 he had a catamaran (he named her *Double Trouble*). Then came *Wave*, a schooner nearly 10 feet longer than *Trouble*. Stevens raced his yachts against whatever competition he could find in New York Harbor and even sailed *Wave* to Boston in search of rivals.

Stevens' example gradually persuaded other rich New Yorkers to build racing craft. And on July 30, 1844, in the cabin of his newest yacht, *Gimcrack*, anchored in New York Harbor off the Battery, Stevens and eight friends met to form the New York Yacht Club. Stevens, not surprisingly, was elected commodore. That same year the club held its first regatta. The members' nine yachts, ranging in size from 16 to 45 tons, raced through the Narrows, which separate Long Island from Staten Island, across the Lower Bay, out to sea around a buoy off Sandy Hook, and back to the harbor. The race was won by the commodore in his new yacht *Cygnet*. During succeeding years the members sailed down Long Island Sound, in what they called "trials of speed," to Huntington, Gardiner's Island and Newport, Rhode Island.

To give the group a base of operations, Commodore Stevens volunteered a one-room frame cottage on the Hudson River shore of his estate as the first clubhouse. And it was in this building in 1850 that the commodore, his brother Edwin and three other members of the club, most of whom had been classmates of the Stevenses at Columbia College, decided to strike a blow at the notion of British yachting supremacy. They would form a syndicate, build a new vessel and take her across the Atlantic the following year to race in England. When the question of who would design her was raised, Stevens had a candidate.

By far the fastest small sailing craft in every American port were the pilot boats—the sleek, fore-and-aft-rigged schooners in which harbor pilots would race far out to sea to meet incoming vessels. The first pilot to reach the new arrival usually got the job of guiding the ship into port. In New York the competition between pilots was particularly fierce, and pilot-boat designers were constantly making modifications and adjustments to their vessels to add speed.

Merrymakers afloat in old Boston

The schooner Dream, flagship of America's first yacht club, threads her way through the congestion of Boston Harbor.

The first yacht club in the United States boasted none of the posh gentility that was later to become the hallmark of such organizations. Founded in the summer of 1834, it was given the modest name of Boston Boat Club by its membership, a loose congregation of exuberant young men who enjoyed boating and playing pranks. It had no burgee or bylaws, and its squadron consisted only of rowboats.

The following summer the members scraped up $2,000 to buy *Dream*, a graceful 46-foot schooner, and elected as their commodore Robert Forbes, a 30-year-old China trader. All summer the Dreamers, as they now called themselves, reveled in day sails, cruises, picnics and gambling parties.

The next year the group acquired a second yacht, the 52-foot schooner *Breeze*, and in the first American yacht club race on record *Dream* beat the new boat to Marblehead. But Forbes, on the *Breeze*, still put one over on the winners: He invited the Dreamers to lunch aboard the new yacht, then inveigled his guests' cook into sneaking their provisions down the *Breeze's* forward hatch. Unknowingly, the men of the *Dream* fed heartily on their own lunch. Later, as the boats raced back home, the laughing commodore compounded the Dreamers' indignation by hoisting one of their empty champagne bottles high up his main gaff.

Such high jinks ended with the financial panic in 1837. Forbes returned to China and the club broke up. Nevertheless, American yachting can trace a kind of genealogical continuity from this first club, because *Dream* was bought by George Schuyler, a New Yorker who was later one of the founders of the New York Yacht Club and who, in 1851, helped form the syndicate that built and raced the famed *America*.

Stevens happened to know a young pilot-boat designer who had the reputation of being both inventive and successful. His name was George Steers. Then 30, Steers had learned the trade in the yard of his father, an English shipwright who had emigrated from Devonshire to America. Young George had little formal education, but displayed a genius for mathematics and design at an early age. In 1836, when he was only 16 years old, he designed and raced a 16-foot sailboat that was so fast it crossed the finish line three miles ahead of the champion racer of the time. It was then that he first met Stevens, who presented the cup for the race. Two years later Steers designed and built a racing shell that he named *John C. Stevens.*

By the time the New York Yacht Club was founded, Steers had designed yachts for three of the charter members (including Stevens). These were all good boats, but what particularly caught Stevens' attention was a pilot boat that Steers had built for one of New York's most venerable seamen, a skipper named Richard Brown. Old Dick Brown gave Steers his head, and the young designer, like his counterparts who were building clipper ships, turned away from the bluff-bowed vessels of earlier years and designed a sleek vessel with a sharp bow and clean run. Steers's little schooner, *Mary Taylor*, promptly outsailed all the other pilot boats in New York, and like her namesake, an entertainer who had danced the "scandalous polka" at Niblo's Gardens in 1844, she gave a performance that was every sailor's delight. After seeing *Mary Taylor* in action, Commodore Stevens had his own 92-foot centerboard yacht *Maria*, which had been designed by his brother Robert, rebuilt at the bow along the lines of the new Steers pilot boat. These modifications were a definite improvement.

Thus it happened that when the time came for Stevens' syndicate to build a yacht to take to England, the members turned to shipbuilder William Brown (no relation to the pilot-boat captain). Brown's designer was George Steers.

The syndicate drove a hard bargain. George L. Schuyler, a member of the group who was in the shipping business, represented his colleagues in dealing with Brown, and dictated a contract that read like a yachtsman's pipe dream. Under the terms of the agreement, the syndicate was not obliged to accept the new yacht unless she was "faster than any vessel in the United States brought to compete with her." Not only that, Brown also agreed that "you are to have the right, instead of accepting her at that time, to send her to England, match her against anything of her size built there, and if beaten still to reject her altogether." Clearly William Brown had to have great faith in designer Steers to agree to such a one-sided contract. And the syndicate expressed its members' confidence in Steers by agreeing to a price of $30,000, a huge sum to pay for a yacht in 1850.

Following the standard designers' practices of the day, George Steers first whittled out a model, reshaping and refining it until he had precisely what he wanted. Then he took off the model's lines and scaled them up to the full size of the yacht, bending wooden battens that he positioned on the mold-loft floor. Pacing back and forth over these outlines of the yacht-to-be, Steers would slide one batten in one direction and

John Cox Stevens, portrayed here at the end of his 11-year stint as the first commodore of the New York Yacht Club, was infatuated with fast sailing yachts all his life. As a youth on his family's Hudson River estate at Hoboken, New Jersey, he often engaged in impromptu races with commercial boats.

nudge another an inch or two the other way, moving them back and forth until he had exactly the right shape. He then nailed the battens to the mold-loft floor, and the yardsmen began cutting timbers to match them.

The vessel that evolved somewhat resembled his pilot schooner *Mary Taylor*. But the new yacht was longer and, despite that, even slimmer than his previous radical designs. Steers started construction in November of 1850. By December the yacht's ribs were poking into the air above William Brown's yard at the foot of 12th Street on the East River.

But the winter of 1850-1851 was bitterly cold, and the shed in which the yacht was being built offered inadequate protection for the ship-wrights. It soon became obvious that Steers and Brown were not going to make the delivery date of April 1, 1851. The syndicate agreed to a month's extension, although that meant there would be little time for trials in the United States before the yacht would have to sail for England for the summer racing season.

It was while waiting anxiously for the vessel's completion that Commodore Stevens received his letter from Lord Wilton inviting the New

Yorkers to visit the Royal Yacht Squadron's clubhouse at Cowes. Stevens had hoped the British would make just such an overture, and he made the most of it. He accepted immediately with "warmest thanks," adding that if the syndicate's new yacht should answer "the sanguine expectations of her builder, and fulfill the stipulations he has made, we propose to avail ourselves of your friendly bidding and take with good grace the sound thrashing we are likely to get by venturing our longshore craft on your rough waters."

Stevens' excessive modesty did not reflect any new doubts about the ability of George Steers so much as it served another purpose. Certainly it had not escaped Stevens' sharp eye that Lord Wilton's letter had been quite carefully phrased: While it was unequivocally an invitation to visit the clubhouse of the Royal Yacht Squadron, it never specifically suggested a race between the two clubs. Wilton's reference to his club's interest in "any improvements in shipbuilding" the Americans could offer might be interpreted as a challenge, but it still left plenty of room for the Englishmen to demur.

There was a good reason for Wilton's restraint. Yacht racing, in both England and the United States in the mid-19th Century, frequently involved more than sport. The usual match was for a large wager, with the American yachtsmen extending public challenges to one another in the pages of such sporting journals as the Spirit of the Times. There was nearly as much betting among yacht owners as among horse owners. Indeed, the New York Yacht Club syndicate regarded its venture as potentially a money-making proposition. Stevens and his partners were not out after silver cups; they were out to bet, and win, more money than they would spend on their yacht.

So Lord Wilton had been cautious not to commit any of the squadron's members, at least until they had a chance to size up this new yacht. And for the same reason, Commodore Stevens had probably replied as he did in hopes of eliciting a response closer to a challenge. Wilton did not take the bait, but Stevens and the other syndicate members proceeded with their plans, confident that they would surely find boats to race against in England, the very cradle of yachting.

Their handsome new yacht was finally delivered in early May, 12 days after her latest deadline. She was beautifully proportioned: 102 feet long overall, 89 feet long at the water line, with a 22½-foot beam and an 11-foot draft. A schooner, the vessel's two masts were raked sharply aft, the mainmast with topmast towering some 96 feet above the deck and the foremast about 27 feet shorter. Adding to the impression of long leanness made by the lines of her hull were a bowsprit that reached 17 feet 6 inches ahead of her bow and a long main boom that swung out 18 feet 3 inches beyond her stern. Her classic schooner rig carried 5,263 square feet of tightly woven canvas duck sail. Belowdecks she was comfortably appointed with generous sleeping quarters for the crew and two saloons that were finished in carved rosewood, polished American walnut and green silk velvet. Perhaps her most distinguishing characteristic was the wide, round cockpit cut in the deck near her stern, which came to be regarded as her trademark. No one seems to know who first thought of her name. Presumably all were in agreement that, consid-

Steam-powered family that sailed into yachting history

It was no accident that yacht racing began its 19th Century rise to popularity at about the same time that working sail embarked on its voyage to oblivion in a cloud of steamboat smoke. The same steam-powered Industrial Revolution that eventually made commercial sailing vessels obsolete also gave people more money to spend on sailing for sport. Proof of this relationship was neatly packaged in a single American family that was immensely influential in both the development of steam-driven transportation and the growth of yacht racing: the Stevens family of Hoboken, New Jersey.

The patriarch of this remarkable household was Colonel John Stevens (right), a lawyer, businessman, self-taught inventor and tireless proponent of progress—especially progress that made him richer. And he sired four talented sons whom he imbued with the same unbounded energy.

Colonel Stevens' chief enthusiasm was the steam engine; on his bedside table he kept the published works of James Watt, the Scottish inventor who patented the first modern condensing steam engine in 1769. Stevens improved upon Watt's engine, and built a boat for it as well—a 100-foot side-wheeler that he named the *Phoenix* (opposite). When he demonstrated her in June 1809, he was just 22 months too late to lay claim to being first in the water with a practical steamboat, for in 1807 Robert Fulton had successfully run the historic *Clermont* up and down the Hudson River.

But Stevens became the first to operate a steamboat on the open sea, when he took the *Phoenix* around the New Jersey peninsula to Philadelphia. There he inaugurated what was to become a lucrative ferry service between Philadelphia and Trenton, and put his sons Robert and Edwin in charge.

The colonel then turned to the use of steam on land. In 1825 he constructed the first American-built locomotive and showed it off on a wooden track in his backyard. In 1830, when the New Jersey Assembly granted him a charter for a line from Perth Amboy to Camden, he was ready. So was his son Robert, who, while whittling, came up with the T rail, the design that when rolled in steel provided the first railroad track strong enough to support heavy loads.

Steam transportation spread rapidly. By midcentury, steamboats were regularly plying American waters, and steam trains rolled over some 9,000 miles of track—all built with Robert's patented T rail. By then, too, steam power had helped to make the Stevenses a very rich family.

In the meantime, another of the colonel's indefatigable sons was in the vanguard of those many captains of industry who discovered that money made on steam could be happily spent on sail. He was John Cox Stevens (page 36), who, as a member of the syndicate that in 1851 built and raced the immortal schooner *America*, bequeathed to the modern sport of yacht racing its most spirited contest and most coveted trophy: the America's Cup.

Colonel John Stevens often stayed up all night working on his inventions—even when he was in his seventies.

Robert Stevens' iron T rail played a vital role in making railroading practical. The flat top provided a smooth surface for carriage wheels, and the flanged bottom could be spiked to wooden crossties.

Colonel John Stevens' Phoenix raises steam as she moves at nine miles per hour off the New Jersey coast. Her 1809 ocean voyage from New York to Delaware Bay was a milestone achievement, for, as one observer exclaimed, "no sea had ever known the domination of steam."

Belching a cloud of sooty smoke, Colonel Stevens' steam wagon chugs around a small loop of track at his estate in Hoboken in 1825. The engine drove a cogged center wheel, which meshed with grooves in the center track to push the car along at six miles per hour.

ering her mission abroad, no name could be more suitable than *America*.

She was christened and quickly put to the test. Her trial horse was to be Stevens' rebuilt yacht *Maria*, which also had Steers's innovative prow and flew 2,500 more square feet of canvas than *America* over a lighter hull. (*Maria* was so light for her sails, in fact, that in a strong breeze she heeled over until her hatches were awash, and Stevens, consequently, rarely ventured to sail her outside of New York Harbor.) On May 14 and again on the following day, *America* effortlessly breezed past *Maria* over a predetermined course. In the third trial the new yacht sprung the head of her foremast and lost her main gaff, letting *Maria* win the day. Still, it appeared from these trials that *America* was clearly the faster of the two. But a few days later the syndicate received dismaying news. Commodore Stevens sent a letter to *The New York Herald* stating that *Maria* had been handicapped during the first two races, in the first by running aground and in the second by an improperly positioned centerboard. In a subsequent letter George Schuyler, who had acted as umpire for the trials, upheld Stevens' contention and declared the two yachts virtually an even match.

The syndicate was shocked. But *America*'s new owners were confronting a dilemma. Time was running short, and it was clear that the

Carved half-hull models of fast sailboats and of the huge steam frigate Niagara line the New York workroom of George Steers, designer of America. The newspaper that commissioned this engraving in 1856 memorialized Steers, who met an untimely death in a carriage accident at the age of 36, as "the greatest of our shipbuilders—the civil hero of our naval fame."

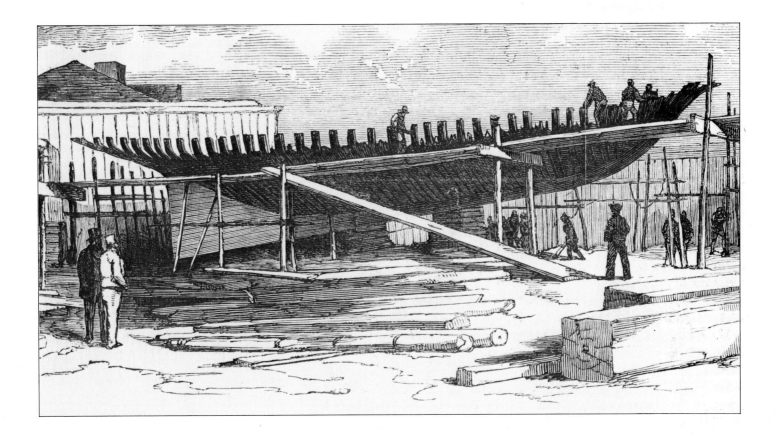

America's clean-lined hull takes shape on the building stocks at William Brown's East River shipyard as workmen race to complete her by their April 1, 1851, deadline. By that date, the builder had promised, the yacht was to be finished "in the best manner, coppered, equipped with joiner's work and rigged for ocean sailing." But he missed the completion date by more than a month.

New York Yacht Club would have to settle for *America* or abandon the entire project. Schuyler made a new proposition to Brown. The syndicate would release him from his promise regarding *America's* performance in return for his reducing her price by a third. Brown had little choice. If he held out for his full construction fee, *America* might lose to *Maria,* or some other vessel, in a new series of trials. Reluctantly, he accepted $20,000 in cash.

The new owners immediately readied their yacht for the transatlantic voyage. *America's* hull was painted gray with a heavy lead paint to inhibit fouling. Her light racing sails were stowed and a suit of heavy working sails borrowed from the schooner *Mary Taylor* went onto her booms. A supply of gin and beer for the crossing was packed aboard. Stevens also prepared for the entertaining he expected to be doing in England. Several cases of brandy and rum went into *America's* hold and, for special occasions, a hamper with two dozen bottles of 50-year-old Madeira "from the celebrated cellar of the late Mr. Bingham of Philadelphia" was carried aboard. More fine wines would be picked up in France, at Le Havre, where *America* would stop for refitting before crossing the English Channel to Cowes. The liquor supply would soon become a source of contention.

To acquire a first-rate skipper for *America,* the syndicate again borrowed from the pilot schooner *Mary Taylor*—in this case her captain, Dick Brown. He in turn chose an able first mate, a second mate and a crew of eight. Several members of the syndicate were to take part in the races as members of the yacht's afterguard—those who rode in the cockpit with the helmsman. They were expected to make the crossing aboard *America*, but just before sailing time, syndicate member Schuyler found that urgent business problems would prevent his going to England. Two other members also decided to stay home—one because of his health and the other because he was no yachtsman—and the remaining members of the afterguard decided to take a faster, more comfortable steamer to France. They offered their places aboard the yacht to designer Steers, who in turn invited his brother James and James's two sons, aged 15 and 17, to join him.

At 8 a.m., June 21, 1851, with the sailing season already under way at Cowes, *America's* lines were cast off from her wharf at the foot of 12th Street. There was scarcely any wind, so a steamer towed her down the East River, through the Upper Bay, the Narrows and the Lower Bay. There she was cast free to make her own way on the 3,200-mile voyage across the Atlantic.

America proved herself seaworthy from the start. As she crossed Sandy Hook bar at 3 o'clock that afternoon, the breeze piped up and sent her racing along at 11 knots. She moved well, taking little water over her bow and driving ahead with none of the pitching to be expected from a 100-foot schooner on the open Atlantic. But she did roll somewhat as the ocean's sweeping swells moved under her hull, and the motion shortly began to get to the second mate. George Steers's brother James had decided to keep a journal of the voyage; one of the first notations was that the mate "turned in rather squamish." By 10 that evening they were moving through a thick fog bank, with the swash of the sea and the creak of the masts echoing back at them. James Steers noted that not only the second mate but the captain and Chips, the carpenter, "took a little brandy and water" to warm their blood.

James Steers was already feeling a bit self-righteous because the ship's motion was not bothering him, and recorded with ill-disguised pleasure that by midnight tough old Captain Brown, along with the mate and carpenter, "took a seidlitz powder"—a mild, effervescent cathartic—although whether this was made necessary by seasickness or by the brandy is not indicated. By 6 a.m. the wind had dropped to six knots, the air was, James wrote, "thick as mush" and the fog "like rain." The cook, as well as James Steers, happily suffered no ill effects, so James could report that on the first full day at sea he enjoyed "a small roast turkey and green peas, boiled beef and pork with a bread pudding to top off with."

On June 23 the fog blew away before a strong breeze, and *America* surged ahead again. Captain Brown had brought along a square sail that, attached to a yard and hoisted on the foremast, would help speed the schooner along when the wind was astern. A schooner, with its fore-and-aft sails, can point up better and sail faster close to the wind than a square-rigged vessel can; but when a vessel is running before the wind nothing draws like a square sail. Brown called *America's* new sail "Big Ben," and ordered it raised for the first time. It bellied out before the wind; the men hauled the braces taut, and all sails, in James's phrase, "set like a board." The schooner went driving east at 12 knots.

Shortly, however, the wind hauled forward of the beam. Big Ben thundered and flapped and had to be lowered. Still the yacht made good time, and James celebrated with "a drink to all our friends at home"—before tucking into another hearty dinner: "veal potpie and Indian fritters with sauce." By evening the wind had shifted once more and Brown was able to raise the square sail again; *America* clipped off an impressive 284 miles in 24 hours.

America, James concluded after five days of brisk winds had carried them across 1,150 miles of ocean, "is the best sea boat that ever went out of the Hook. The way we have passed every vessel we have seen must be witnessed to be believed."

Even when the wind dropped they made relatively good time. In a light breeze on June 28, they eased past the British bark *Clyde*, bound out of New York for Liverpool. At 10 a.m. she had risen before them on the horizon, and by 6 p.m. she was hull down astern.

On June 30 the wind increased. Brown kept all sails set, and *America* breezed past another ship. By 8 a.m. on July 1, the yacht, for the first time, began to pitch, so much that her bowsprit was dipping below the waves. The combination of rolling and plunging finally proved too much for *America*'s designer, and his brother sympathetically recorded that George Steers "could eat no dinner." Even James began to complain:

Tufted velvet upholstery and carved rosewood paneling adorn the spacious aft cabin of America in this watercolor cutaway by Pehr Cedergren, a Swedish marine artist who went to London in 1851 to study shipbuilding innovations. Cedergren made some 70 technical sketches of the American yacht. They were later used to build the first Swedish racing yacht, named Sverige, which then lost to her prototype in a race in 1852 on the Solent.

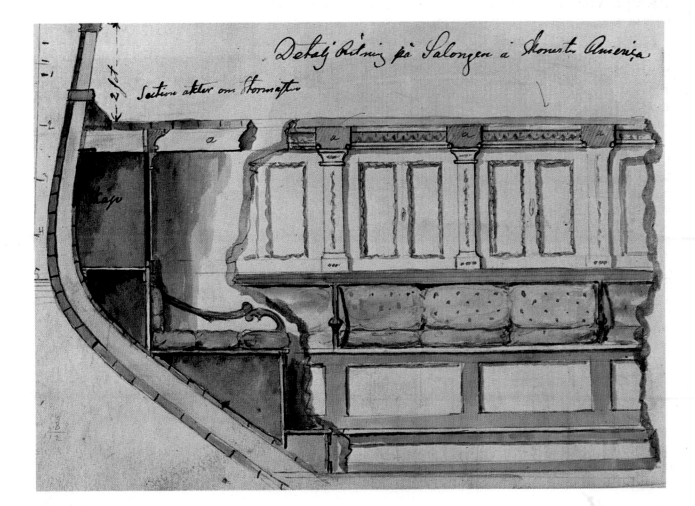

"Should I live to get home, this will be my last sea trip. All my clothes are wet. It has rained every day since we left." (Dinner: "fried ham and eggs, boiled corn-beef, mashed potatoes and rice pudding.") The wind increased, and Dick Brown drove the schooner hard. On July 3, in a howling night, the wind carried away the binding of the starboard foreshrouds, endangering the support of the foremast. Brown hove her to, lowered the foresail and sailed through the night under main and jib, with the foremast held in place by the halyards that had been rigged for Big Ben, the square sail. In daylight next morning, the captain brought the schooner up into the wind again, and a daring seaman inched up the swaying ratlines to rebind the shrouds.

On July 4, appropriately, the sun reappeared, the fog cleared, *America* moved along briskly before a fine breeze, and all aboard enjoyed their national holiday, "the glory of all true hearted Americans," James wrote. Captain Brown canceled all but the most essential work and issued a bottle of gin to the men from the crew's liquor supply. George perked up. Later that day the breeze died and George again sank into a depression. His brother took the extreme measure of trying to cheer him up by standing him in the yacht's big round cockpit and dousing him with buckets of sea water. It did not seem to help. "His appetite is poor," wrote James, to whom this was a grave symptom indeed.

Through the next four days the calm hung over them like a cloud, the yacht rolling and her sails "slatting enough to tear them to pieces." But they were cheered by the knowledge that they were close to the English Channel. Ships were all around them: Four were visible from the deck at various times during one day, and two more were sighted from the masthead. Even George Steers's despondency began to lift. And, on July 8, when a west wind at last came up, James exulted. *America*, he wrote, "commenced stepping along pretty lively, which I can tell you was gratifying to all on board."

That afternoon Captain Brown set the square sail again, and the yacht picked up even more speed. Among the ships in sight was a large merchantman with every sail set, including her royals. "We passed her," James crowed, "like leaving a dock."

The fresh breeze held, but a problem loomed: "Our liquor is all but gone." The next day James wrote, "We had a glorious run these last 24 hours." But "we had to break open one of the boxes marked RUM," belonging to Commodore Stevens. "George had the bellyache and all our own was consumed," James explained. "We were not going to starve in a market place, so we took four bottles out and I think it will last us." Two days later they sighted land—one of the Scilly Isles, off the southwestern coast of England—and by the evening of July 11, *America* was lying to off Le Havre; Captain Brown had prudently waited for daylight, since the harbor has a 24-foot tide. "We have made the run from the foot of Twelfth Street to Le Havre," James wrote, "in 20 days and six hours."

At 10 o'clock in the morning on July 12, *America* dropped anchor inside the harbor. It had been an extremely fast passage for a yacht of 102 feet, especially considering the fact that *America* had been becalmed for five days. On every one of six days when she had had good wind, she had made 200 miles or more.

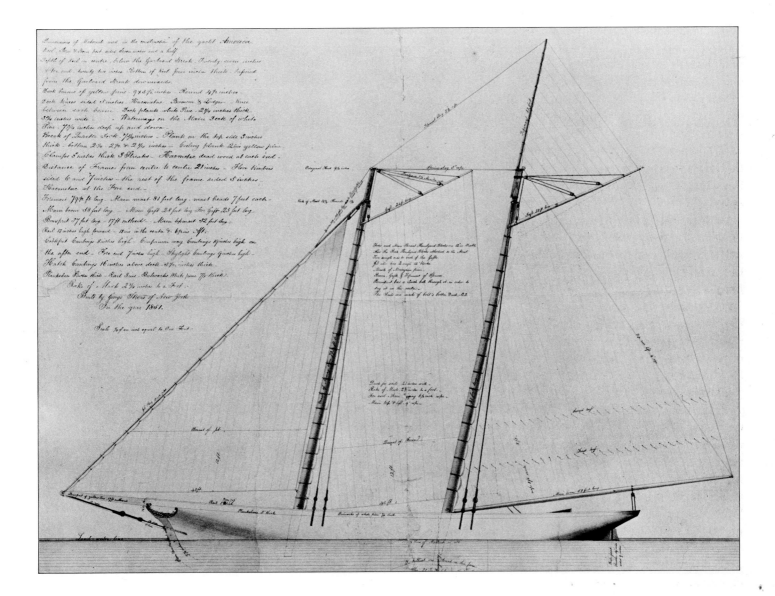

America's canvas, as seen in this sail plan, was sewed up from 22-inch-wide strips of tightly woven, machine-made cotton duck. Her sails were superior to those of her English competitors, which were made of loosely woven flax in the belief that a light, billowing fabric would better capture the wind.

But the steamer packets were somewhat faster, and three syndicate members—Commodore Stevens, his brother Edwin and Colonel James Hamilton—were waiting in Paris. There Colonel Hamilton had an unsettling encounter with an American friend fresh from London, Horace Greeley, editor of *The New York Tribune*. Greeley had been visiting the Great Exhibition in its Crystal Palace, and he was opposed to any U.S.-British race. His conversation with Hamilton was a revealing example of the still-defensive spirit of the young United States.

"The eyes of the world are on you," Greeley warned Hamilton. "You will be beaten, and the country will be abused." Hamilton tried to explain that it was too late to turn back: "We are in for it, and we must go." Greeley's response surprised him: "Well, if you go and are beaten, you had better not return to your country."

Hamilton had previously been advised against *America's* challenge by the U.S. Minister to France, William Rives; but Greeley's warning seemed excessive. Hamilton reflected later that it "awakened me to the deep and extended interest our enterprise had excited, and the responsibility we had assumed. It did not, however, induce us to hesitate. I remembered that our packet ships had outrun theirs, and why should not this schooner, built upon the best model?"

The warning nevertheless struck home. Hamilton and Stevens spared no effort in preparing the yacht for the races to come. While Hamilton prepared to go ahead to Cowes to scout the potential opposition, Commodore Stevens and his brother went down to Le Havre with the Steers brothers to supervise the yacht's refit for racing.

America was nudged into a dry dock and her copper bottom was scraped and polished. Her forefoot, the joint between stem and keel, was planed down slightly, and a few inches were shaved from her rudder. Her topsides were given a fresh coat of gleaming black paint, with a gold stripe, and the eagle on her counter was painted gold. The heavy working sails came off her booms, and the light cotton sails were bent on. By July 29, *America* was ready for her first test against an English yacht— and it came sooner than expected.

George and James Steers and James's sons had left Le Havre a few days earlier, taking the Channel steamer to Southampton. By July 30 they were on the Isle of Wight watching for the yacht. So, apparently, was nearly everyone else on the island. The latest steamer from Le Havre had brought word that *America* was on the way. Going down to the beach early in the morning, the Steerses spotted her, anchored in the roadstead about six miles away from Cowes. They were on the point of hiring a boatman to take them out to her when they noticed that the sails were inching up her masts.

Commodore Stevens and Captain Brown had been aboard the yacht when she crossed the Channel, and as they approached the roadstead off Cowes they had been blanketed by a thick bank of fog that obscured the island. They anchored for the night. By dawn the fog was lifting, but now they were becalmed in an adverse tide. Shortly, however, a breeze stirred across the water, and the Americans noticed a sleek cutter gliding down toward them.

Stevens made out the name painted on her transom: *Lavrock*. He had heard of her—she was one of the newest and fastest yachts in the Royal Yacht Squadron. It soon became apparent that *Lavrock's* owner was eager for an impromptu race. Instead of coming alongside and hailing *America*, the cutter slowly tacked back and forth ahead of her, waiting for her anchor to come up.

Commodore Stevens was in a difficult spot. *America* was loaded with provisions, and was four to five inches deeper in the water than she should have been for racing trim. Looking through his glass at the roadstead and the island, Stevens could see that all the "yachts and vessels in the harbor, the wharfs, and windows of all the houses bordering on them, were filled with thousands of spectators, watching with eager eyes the eventful trial they saw we could not escape: for the *Lavrock* stuck to us, sometimes laying to, and sometimes tacking," taunting *America* and spoiling for a race.

The breeze had increased to a steady five knots. And while the American yacht was not yet in racing trim, Stevens noted that *Lavrock* was towing her dinghy, perhaps as a gesture of similar dishabille. In any case, there was no way for *America* to avoid this first challenge. "We got up our sails with heavy hearts," Stevens recalled, "after waiting until we were ashamed to wait longer."

Lavrock was about 200 yards in front as *America's* sails finally caught the breeze and began to pull the schooner forward against the ebbing tide. "For the first five minutes," Stevens remembered, "not a sound was heard, save, perhaps, the beating of our anxious hearts, or the slight ripple of the water." Old Dick Brown crouched in *America's* round cockpit, guiding the yacht, his hand lightly holding her long tiller. "The men were motionless as statues," Stevens recalled, "with their eager eyes fastened upon the *Lavrock* with a fixedness and intensity that seemed almost supernatural."

It took only those still, tense five minutes to tell. *America,* with her tightly woven sails drawing the freshening breeze, "worked quickly and surely to windward" of *Lavrock.* "The crisis was past," Stevens said; and as if everyone had held his breath for a full five minutes, "some dozens of deep-drawn sighs proved that the agony was over." *America* eased past *Lavrock* and rounded up off Cowes Castle nearly a third of a mile in the lead, before the assembled multitude on the island, including members of the Royal Yacht Squadron. Only "twenty minutes after our anchor was down," Stevens recollected, "the Earl of Wilton was on board to welcome and introduce us to his friends."

Stevens' jubilation, however, was short-lived. It quickly became clear that the *America* syndicate's purpose of making money by wagering large sums on the races would have been better served if she had lost to *Lavrock.* Now that she had beaten one of the Royal Yacht Squadron's fastest new cutters, in full view of all the yachtsmen at Cowes, *America* found no challengers.

Stevens dispatched a courteous note to the Royal Yacht Squadron, welcoming a match with any member. He received no reply. He attempted to enter the annual regatta of the Royal Victoria Yacht Club at Ryde, near Cowes, and was politely informed that the regatta was open only to yachts owned singly, not by a syndicate. Angry and frustrated, he sailed *America* alongside the other yachts in this race, veering off after passing

This grand American eagle with a nine-foot wingspread adorned America's stern at Cowes, but disappeared in 1858 while the boat was laid up for repairs near London. Some years later, members of the Royal Yacht Squadron found the emblem above the portal of The Eagle pub on the Isle of Wight and rescued it. It then decorated the squadron's clubhouse until 1912, when it was given to the New York Yacht Club.

most of them—thereby diminishing even further any chances of a challenge. As the days went by and the British yachtsmen remained impassive, Stevens took the initiative and sent off to Lord Wilton at the Royal Yacht Squadron a challenge of his own on behalf of the syndicate: *America* would race any yacht of any size, except in winds of less than six knots, for the enormous wager of 10,000 guineas (about $50,000)—enough to build at least two yachts her size. "This was a staggerer for them all," James Steers wrote in his journal. Yet even so daring a taunt did not bring a response.

Meanwhile a storm was brewing aboard *America*. Relations between the Steers brothers and Commodore Stevens were deteriorating. The commodore regarded the brothers as skilled artisans of a social order somewhat lower than his. For their part, the Steerses, in the true American spirit, considered themselves Stevens' equal and were outraged at his cavalier treatment of them. "He is a damned old hog, bristles and all," James groused.

The commodore, moreover, had been less than pleased at discovering the drain on his rum, and was considerably irked to find that it continued. More infuriating, he was unable to find even a trace of his treasured supply of 50-year-old Madeira. James had at least part of the answer. As he casually described it: "We take about two bottles of rum every day. At night he sits down on the cabin floor in his shirt tail and counts them all over. When he finds any missing he calls the steward and says: 'Where the hell does my liquor go to?' He (steward) says: 'I don't know, sir. The Messrs Steers take some when they want any.' 'How do they get it when I carry the key?' " The solution to the mystery was simple enough: The Steerses had had the foresight to make their own key.

As relations worsened, the Steerses finally decided to go home. Although they had had a free trip to Cowes, they were taking time that they should have been spending in the shipyard in New York, during the busiest season. They went to Stevens and told him they were leaving and why. Stevens was surprised, but evidently not overly displeased. When 15-year-old Henry Steers begged to stay, his father agreed to leave him in the care of Captain Brown. As for Brown's reaction to the departure, James reported, "Dick looked as though he had lost all his friends." The Steers brothers and James's other son packed their things. Dick Brown "came ashore with us and we took a parting drink." And *America's* designer left for home only four days before the race that would make his creation the most celebrated yacht in history.

Abandoned by his designer and frustrated by his reluctant hosts, Commodore Stevens discovered an unlikely ally in the British press. The yachting correspondent for *The Times of London*, writing about the arrival of the visitor from America, chided British yachtsmen in a picturesque metaphor.

"Most of us have seen the agitation which the appearance of a sparrowhawk in the horizon creates among a flock of woodpigeons or skylarks, when unsuspecting all danger, and engaged in airy flights or playing about over the fallows, they all at once come down to the ground and are rendered almost motionless by fear of the disagreeable visitor." *America's* arrival, *The Times* reporter continued, had had a

The Earl of Wilton, commodore of the Royal Yacht Squadron, opened the squadron's 1851 Hundred Guinea Cup race to yachts of "all rigs and all nations" as a gesture of hospitality to foreigners visiting the Great Exhibition in London that year. But the only non-British vessel to compete was America.

similar effect: It "seems to have been completely paralyzing." Will Britain's yachtsmen, he asked, "allow the illustrious stranger to return with the proud boast to the New World that she had flung down the gauntlet to England, Ireland and Scotland, and that no one had been found to take it up?" If so, he darkly hinted, "there will be some question as to the pith and courage of our men, and yachting must sink immeasurably in public estimation."

There was more in the same vein, and it finally stung the Englishmen into action. August 22 was the occasion of the squadron's annual race around the Isle of Wight, this year being run for the club's One Hundred Guinea Cup, and Lord Wilton and the Royal Yacht Squadron invited *America* to compete. It was a wide-open race for yachts of all sizes, rigs and nationalities, with no handicap: a veritable free-for-all, and hardly what the *America* syndicate had in mind. They wanted a race against one yacht for sizable stakes. The squadron's regatta would bring out more than a dozen yachts, forcing *America* to sail against an entire fleet, and for a trophy rather than for cash.

Stevens realized that entering such a race could be counterproductive. If *America* won, it would be even more difficult, probably impossible, for the syndicate to find a challenger for a match race. But it was the only offer the syndicate had received, so Commodore Stevens entered the race. And when a few days later an Englishman finally accepted Stevens' call for a two-boat contest, there was no graceful way for the syndicate to withdraw from the contest for the Hundred Guinea Cup.

This new challenger was Robert Stephenson, a 47-year-old Member of Parliament, railroad tycoon and owner of *Titania*, a modern 100-ton schooner with an iron hull. Stephenson, it happened, was a friend of Commodore Stevens' and had visited him during business trips to New York. Now he stepped forward to accept his American friend's challenge, and it was agreed that they would race in the Channel on August 28 for the modest wager of £100. But first, Stevens had to take on all comers in the regatta.

The 53-mile course around the diamond-shaped Isle of Wight (page 52) was, as the London *Times* had noted, "notoriously one of the most unfair to strangers that can be selected." The paper went on to explain that "the currents and tides render local knowledge of more value than swift sailing and nautical skill." The Solent and Spithead, two bodies of water that separate the island from the Hampshire mainland, both have strong tides that eddy and race over innumerable shoals and rocks. No fewer than 15 lights that marked dangerous areas encircled the island in 1851. Indeed, British yachtsmen in these waters knew that some shoals could be crossed only in a stiff breeze at high tide, with the yacht heeled well over so that her keel was at an angle. The winner of a race often was the skipper who knew just where he could slip through a treacherous patch of shallows, so close to the bottom that the local phrase for the maneuver was "cracking the crabs' backs."

Partly for this reason, Stevens decided to hire a local pilot. Robert Underwood was recruited by the U.S. consul in Southampton. James Steers, who met Underwood before leaving for home, described him as "a fine old 'sojer,' who can take his pint of ale and not wink at it," an adequate recommendation in James's opinion. Through Underwood, Stevens met a Cowes sailmaker, George Ratsey, who designed a jib boom for *America,* on which she would carry an extra flying jib forward of the others to help her to windward. Old Dick Brown grumbled that there was no need for the additional rig. But Stevens insisted, the jib boom was added to *America's* bowsprit, and she was pronounced ready to try for the Hundred Guinea Cup.

There was a light drizzle on the morning of Friday, August 22, 1851. But the clouds soon moved away and the sun emerged, accompanied by a five-knot breeze. By midmorning the waterfront was swarming with expectant crowds. Wrote a reporter for the British periodical *Bell's Life:* "In the memory of man Cowes never presented such an appearance as on this day." Colorful booths had sprung up during the night. Countless hawkers—and, no doubt, pickpockets—passed through the throng. Yachts in the Solent, and even some of the villas along the shore, were bedecked in lines of fluttering signal flags. The roadstead was nearly as jammed as the esplanade at Cowes, with every manner of craft circling the big yachts.

The challenge from America was the subject of the hour. The *Times* reporter who had chided the reluctant yachtsmen now wrote glowingly: "A large proportion of the peerage and gentry of the United Kingdom forsook the sports of the moors to witness the struggle between the yachtsmen of England, hitherto unmatched and unchallenged, and the Americans who had crossed the Atlantic to meet them." Not that British yachtsmen had lost much of their complacency. The *Times* pointed out that until "the *America* came over, the few who were aware that there was a flourishing club in New York did not regard it as of the slightest consequence, or as at all likely to interfere with their monopoly of the glory of the manliest and most useful of all sports." And the publication *Yacht List* had pontificated that "yacht building is an art in which England was unrivalled, and she is distinguished preeminently and alone for the perfection of science in handling them."

And yet there was an atmosphere of uneasy anticipation. One spectator reported that on the train from London to Southampton no one talked about anything but the American challenger. Along the shore and in the boats offshore everyone flocked to study the black-hulled visitor riding at anchor off the Royal Yacht Squadron clubhouse at Cowes. She was unmistakable with her sharp bow and raked masts amid the bluff-bowed schooners and cutters of the British yachtsmen. In the clubhouse, reported one journalist, "gentlemen sit at the windows or in the porch with telescope to eye staring at the phenomenon." "Here is the gage thrown down to the whole kingdom," trumpeted *The Times.* Crusty old Lord Anglesey had a pithier comment: "If she is right," he remarked, "all of us are wrong."

That morning 15 vessels made their way to the starting line and anchored in two ranks, cutters in the first and schooners 300 yards behind them. (Regattas of this size in the 1850s started from anchor; a fleet of such huge craft maneuvering for a running start would have created impossible confusion.) The entrants ranged in size from the little 47-ton cutter *Aurora* to the awesome 392-ton, three-masted schooner *Brilliant*. The schooner *America*, at 171 tons, was a middle-sized vessel in this company. All were in position by 9:30 a.m. Precisely at 9:55 the cannon at the Royal Yacht Squadron's clubhouse boomed and sent up a cloud of smoke—the preparatory signal. Amid a screeching of blocks, the sails fluttered up the masts of the yachts. On both sides of the starting line a huge fleet of spectator craft started along the course, eastward along the shore of the Isle of Wight and toward the Channel. Five minutes later came the second cannon, signaling the start of the race. The yachts' anchors clanked on deck and the cutters and schooners surged ahead— all except *America*.

She was still at anchor. When her sails had risen, she had moved ahead over her anchor and her crew had been unable to hoist it. Captain Brown, with a few choice words, ordered the sails lowered again. *America* fell back; her anchor came up; her sails rose once more; and she took off after the rest of the fleet, well behind the leaders.

The first leg of the 53-mile course was east by southeast down Spithead, which lay between the northeastern shore of the island and the southern coast of the Hampshire mainland. As the flotilla proceeded grandly down the coast, the majestic yachts, surrounded by smaller spectator craft and hissing steamers, made a glorious spectacle. The sight of the hundreds of sails framed against the shimmering blue water moved one onlooker to exclaim that "no other country in the world could exhibit anything like it."

The men aboard *America* were less interested in the picturesque tableau. Their yacht was beginning to pick up speed, and shortly she was passing the laggards. Besides Commodore Stevens, his brother Edwin and Colonel Hamilton, there were 18 others aboard, including Captain Brown, pilot Underwood, some sailors recruited from noncompeting British yachts and the remaining American crew. At Brown's orders, most of them distributed themselves about the deck aft of the foremast for proper balance, and crouched in readiness to jump to their stations. Stevens and his afterguard stood in the big circular cockpit, Brown's hand guiding the yacht's long, delicately balanced tiller. There was no idle conversation above the chuckle of the water alongside and the creak of the rings on the masts.

A few smiles of satisfaction were exchanged, however, as *America* pointed up so well that she passed some of the British yachts to windward. Within a quarter of an hour she had moved through most of the fleet, and had only three yachts ahead of her. But they were holding their pace, especially the leader, *Gypsy Queen*, a 160-ton schooner surging along under towering clouds of sail. In fact, it seemed to Brown as if the leaders were bunched up in order to keep *America* from cutting through them. Running before the wind, *America* jibed to one side and then the other, seeking a clear course between the yachts ahead. Soon the breeze showed signs of dying. Then, as the vanguard was passing Osborne House, the little cutter *Volante*, which *America* had just passed, caught a gust in her huge jib and, being lighter and more responsive to the wind, surged ahead of the entire fleet.

The breeze did not die, however; it picked up. Shortly *America*'s big

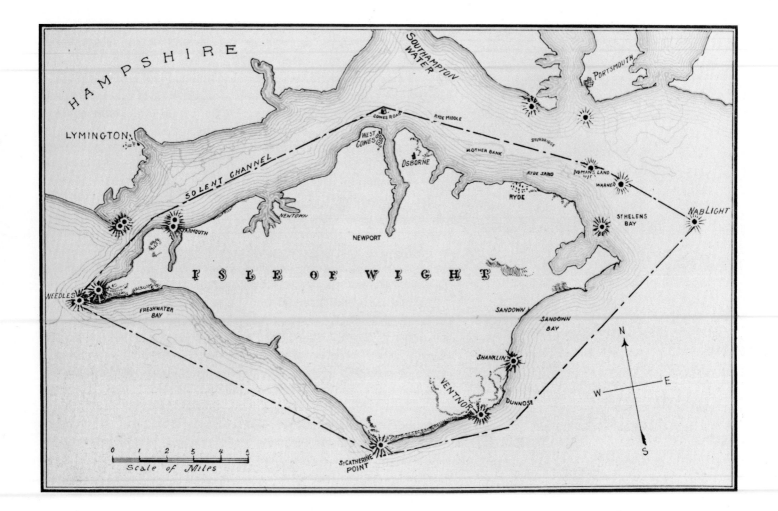

sails grew taut, and the yacht put her shoulder down and went to work. With the water now rushing along her lee bulwark, she overtook the leaders one by one. To the British onlookers crowding the big pier at Ryde near the eastern extremity of the island, *America's* performance was nothing less than spectacular. While the other yachts rose and dipped in the gathering whitecaps, tossing spray halfway up their masts, *America* seemed to cut straight through the waves. But the most impressive contrast was in her sails.

America's raked masts were set slightly forward of the usual mast position for a schooner, permitting her to carry a larger mainsail. More important was the difference between the British and the American sails themselves. British sails, most of them made of hand-woven flax and flown loose-footed—attached to the boom only at each end—spilled much of the wind from their bottom edges as they bellied out, and they were so porous that one could feel a breeze on the lee side of the sailcloth. During the race the crewmen continually doused them to make the cloth shrink and reduce its porosity, thereby making the sails more efficient, but still some of the wind managed to leak through.

America's sails, made of tightly machine-spun cotton duck and laced all along the booms, were taut, nonporous and "as flat as a drumhead,"

The 53-mile course for the 1851 race around the Isle of Wight forms a rough diamond shape. The race started at the top of the diamond and proceeded clockwise. At far right is the Nab, where America took a shortcut by sailing inside the light instead of rounding it—escaping disqualification because the course instructions were ambiguous.

A racing fleet rounds the tall, chalky rocks known as The Needles, at the west end of the Isle of Wight, in this 1836 engraving. Likened to "the lower jawbone of a sea monster, teeth awash," by one sailing writer, The Needles and their encircling eddies were among the worst hazards of the 1851 race; here America lost way in dying winds and a contrary tide.

as one observer put it. So little did they bulge in the wind that one old salt later recalled watching as *America* sailed toward him and being unable to tell, even "with the aid of a spy-glass," whether or not she carried a sail on her main boom; it was so flat that it was completely obscured by the mainmast.

An hour and a half from the start, as the boats neared the eastern tip of the Isle of Wight and were about to enter the open Channel, *America* moved up past the big leaders and then inched past the spirited little *Volante*. With the breeze freshening and a chop building up from the Channel, *America* moved steadily ahead of the fleet. And at this point four of the leading skippers made a costly mistake.

Off the eastern point of the island was a lightship called the Nab, marking a cluster of rocks and indicating the shoal areas between it and the shore of the island. Four of the yachtsmen, following local custom, tacked off to go out around the Nab. *America's* Captain Brown did not.

Before the start of the race, each yacht had been issued instruction cards indicating the course and rules of the race. A program of the race had also been printed, for participants and spectators alike. While the program stated that the course was "outside the Nab," the instruction cards did not include such a specific direction; they simply mentioned the Nab as one of the marks, without indicating on which side the vessel should leave the lightship. There was, of course, the danger of running aground on one of the shoals between the Nab and the shore. But evidently Robert Underwood, the pilot, assured Brown that he knew where the deeper water was, because Brown took *America* inside the mark on a shortcut that saved at least two miles. By the time the other yachts had rounded the Nab, *America* was far ahead of the nearest one. And some of the trailing yachts had caught up with the leaders by following *America* on the same shortcut.

But *America's* luck then changed. The breeze began to die, and a few of the lighter boats started to come up on her. Off the curve of shoreline south of the Nab, a strong tide flowed in toward the beach. *America* was caught in it, with barely enough breeze to keep from being swept onshore. And as she was working her way into safer water, her new jib boom broke.

The boom itself was not at fault; it had easily withstood the light pressure of the wind. But the crew, using a windlass to pull the jib sheet taut, had cranked it in too tight. There was a cracking, splintering sound, and the jib boom curled back over the bowsprit. Dick Brown swore and brought *America* into the wind while the men scrambled out onto the bowsprit. At Brown's orders they jettisoned the jib boom. *America* was brought back on course and out into deeper water, still in the lead, but by a smaller margin.

The winds around the Isle of Wight are predictable only in their unpredictability. In the open Channel south of the island there was less wind than there had been in the sheltered Spithead. *America* kept moving west along the south shore, but the going was slow, and baffling currents kept taking her off course. She was not the only vessel to suffer, however, nor the one to suffer most. An errant current carried the cutter *Arrow* onto a rock ledge east of the island's Mill Bay. Another cutter, *Alarm*, started to her rescue and almost followed her aground. Two other yachts, *Freak* and *Volante*, tacking close to shore, collided; *Volante*, the early leader and one of the fastest in the fleet, lost her entire jib boom and, along with *Alarm* and *Arrow*, now hopelessly behind the rest of the field, had to retire from the race.

By now only three British yachts, *Bacchante*, *Eclipse* and *Aurora*, were giving *America* any competition. Several others were in sight, but far astern of her.

America glided past St. Catherine's Point, at the southern tip of the island, altered her course to northwest and loosened her sheets for a

With her sails set wing and wing— the mainsail to port and the foresail to starboard—America runs by a large spectator fleet for the Cowes Road finish line in this 1851 oil painting by Fitz Hugh Lane. Because she finished so far out in front, said The Times of London, "on every side was heard the hail, 'Is America first?' The answer, 'Yes.' 'What's second?' The reply, 'Nothing.'"

quartering breeze that had begun to look promising. The wind held, and *America* swept up the island's southwest coast, reopening the gap between her and the other vessels. Ahead of her, near the western turning point of the race, a pleasant surprise lay in wait.

Along that shore a row of great chalk and limestone cliffs, not unlike the more famous cliffs of Dover, have over the years broken off and toppled into the sea, forming a jagged jumble of obstructions known as The Needles. The tides sweeping in and out of the Solent surge through these dangerous pinnacles. But inside the treacherous barrier lies a protected cove called Alum Bay. Now, as *America* skimmed along the coast, a black-hulled, gilt-decorated paddle-wheel steamer came swishing and thunking out of the bay. She was the royal yacht *Victoria and Albert*. The Queen had decided to come around the opposite side of the island to meet the yachts.

Commodore Stevens and Captain Dick Brown immediately recognized *Victoria and Albert*, which wheeled about and steamed alongside. As the schooner swept past the royal yacht, the Americans were moved to extend a formal salute—a courtesy that the Queen had never received from her own yachting subjects during the course of a race. *America's* blue-and-white ensign dipped, Stevens, Brown and the rest of the afterguard in the cockpit doffed their yachting caps, and every man in the crew pulled off his hat. It was, the London *Times* reported, "a mark of respect to the Queen not the less becoming because it was bestowed by Republicans."

America rounded the lighthouse marking The Needles. Then the wind began to die, fading into a fickle breeze that fluctuated in direction and scattered cat's-paws across the surface of the sea. The royal steamer went on to the finish line at Cowes—thus missing what turned out to be an unexpectedly exciting last leg of the race.

America had taken seven and a half hours to cover the 41 miles to the Needles Lighthouse. Now, in the shifting wind and against an ebbing Solent tide, she took three hours to complete the last 12 miles of the course, drifting along with her foresail and mainsail goosewinged, one out to port and the other to starboard, in order to present the largest possible surface area of sail to the faint following wind.

Astern of her one cutter came stubbornly on. Little *Aurora* had gone outside the Nab, but continued her dogged pursuit. Now she picked up a shift of wind and began to draw closer. At The Needles she had been all of eight miles astern. But as Stevens, Brown and the rest of *America's* contingent anxiously watched, *Aurora* steadily closed the gap. Dusk was settling over the Solent, darkening the white cliffs and obscuring the finish line. *Aurora's* outline loomed larger and larger behind them like a great avenging bird, her wings red against the horizon in the west. But she was still some distance astern at 8:37 p.m., when the men aboard *America* saw a kaleidoscope of light in the sky just ahead of them, followed by the crackle and burst of fireworks, signaling that *America* had crossed the finish line. Her official time was 10 hours 37 minutes. Little *Aurora* came whisking past the line only 18 minutes after her. Even if the handicapping rule of the time had applied, *America* would have won by two minutes.

LOOK OUT FOR SQUALLS!

A childlike John Bull (right) gapes
in surprise and chagrin as his crude little
boat is beaten by a toy America in this
1851 Punch cartoon. Some Britons blamed
the loss on British officialdom's
conservative attitudes. One writer claimed
facetiously that England had had a
yacht design similar to the American one,
but that "of course, in consequence,
it was thrown out by the Admiralty."

The spectator fleet demonstrated British sportsmanship with a fusillade of guns, whistles, bells and gongs. Throughout the evening, signal cannon were fired as three other yachts straggled in: *Bacchante* at 9:30, *Eclipse* at 9:45, *Brilliant* at 1:20 a.m. The committee boat did not wait for the rest, most of which had dropped out of the race. But more than 6,000 Britons remained at Cowes throughout the evening to watch the fireworks and stare at the yachtsmen as their launches deposited them on the seaweed-covered steps of the Royal Yacht Squadron's pier. Inside the clubhouse genial fellowship prevailed. Squadron members congratulated Commodore Stevens and U.S. Ambassador Abbott Lawrence, who had arrived late and almost missed the race. The Ambassador diplomatically replied that "though he could not but be proud of the triumph of his fellow citizens, he still felt it was but the children giving a lesson to the father."

Next day the squadron's race committee had a further opportunity to lean over backward in being fair to the American. George H. Ackers, owner of *Brilliant*, the largest yacht in the race and the last of the official finishers, formally protested *America's* shortcut inside the Nab. The race committee, which could have made a good case that the route of Isle of Wight races customarily went outside the Nab, instead concluded that since the printed race instructions did not specifically mention it, *America* had broken no rule. So Commodore Stevens was formally presented with the Hundred Guinea Cup, an enormous, ornate trophy in the shape of a pitcher.

The Americans, who had expressed their courtly pleasure at the presence of the Queen the previous day, were even more impressed to be told that Her Majesty wished to visit their yacht. Captain Brown, after seeing to it that *America* was in impeccable condition, took the schooner to an anchorage off Osborne House.

At 4 p.m. a royal barge nudged *America's* port gangway, and the Queen, in hoop skirt with a white shawl over her head and accompanied by Prince Albert, regally ascended to the deck. Victoria knew ships and knew what she liked: She did not like sailing ships. She nevertheless examined *America* in detail. Commodore Stevens led her on a tour belowdecks through the yacht's paneled saloons. He answered Her Majesty's questions about the yacht's ballasting and included, at her request, a look at the crew's quarters. Colonel Hamilton, attired for the occasion in morning coat, ruffled shirt and topper, meanwhile escorted Prince Albert about the yacht. Legend has it that Old Dick Brown asked the Prince to wipe his boots before stepping into *America's* freshly scrubbed cockpit. The story is unsubstantiated, but the Queen herself would have understood such a request: She tested the cleanliness of the yacht's galley by wiping a royal handkerchief along a shelf—and expressed her pleasure at finding no dust. Before descending to the royal barge, she saw to it that each member of the crew received a gold sovereign.

Not every Briton joined in the Americans' celebration. "There was an awful crying and moaning about Cowes," young Henry Steers reported later. Much was made of the Americans' employment of a British pilot and crewmen, and a few carpers went so far as to claim that the yacht's designer, George Steers, actually was an Englishman since he had been born of an English emigrant in the U.S.

An even stranger notion was entertained by the salty, peg-legged old Marquess of Anglesey, who came to half believe the claim of his yacht's captain that *America* had a concealed engine and a propeller aft of her rudder. Watching *America*, under jib and mainsail only, sail past the marquess's *Pearl*, the captain said, "Your lordship knows that no vessel with sails alone could do that." As the American yacht slowed in a calm spot, the captain said, "Now the engine is stopped." When a bit of breeze sent *America* forward again, he said, "Now it is going." The marquess asked for permission to come aboard the American yacht. And when Commodore Stevens welcomed him, the 83-year-old man stumped aft, leaned out over the counter to look for a propeller and would have tumbled overboard if Stevens had not grabbed him by his good leg and hauled him back.

Soon, anyone who cared to inspect *America's* hull got the chance when she was hauled out of the water into the Royal Navy's dry dock after the capricious currents of the Solent caused her to brush the bottom and nick her keel. It was a rainy day, and the day before her slated duel with *Titania*, but hundreds of people gathered at the Portsmouth yard to inspect the yacht's slim, shiny undersides. No propeller. When

A great yacht's active old age

During her duty as a training ship for Navy midshipmen, the yacht America lies at anchor in Boston Navy Yard.

The men who built *America* wanted only to make her the fastest sailer afloat. They never dreamed that she would prove extraordinarily durable as well—tough enough, in fact, to withstand almost a century of service, not only as a yacht but as a warship, Navy training vessel and floating museum.

For a decade after her victory at Cowes in 1851, the boat was used for pleasure by a succession of owners in Europe and America. When the Civil War broke out in America, a cashiered Royal Navy officer named Henry Decie took her to Georgia and sold her to the Confederacy. He stayed on at the helm for the yacht's first mission: spiriting Southern agents to England to acquire war supplies. Decie figured, correctly, that Union gunboats would ignore a pleasure yacht. To make doubly sure, he flew the burgee of the Royal Victoria Yacht Club during the Atlantic round trip.

The next year the yacht was scuttled near Jacksonville, Florida, in the face of a Union advance. The Unionists raised her, and for a year the swift *America* stood blockade duty—helping to capture or destroy six ships—and chased Confederate privateers. The Navy used her for a decade after that as a training ship, then sold her in 1873 to a well-known Civil War veteran, General Benjamin Butler of Boston, whose heirs sailed her for pleasure for almost 50 years. In 1921 her aging hull faced demolition, but she was saved by a syndicate of yachtsmen, who rebuilt her for the Navy to berth at Annapolis as a museum ship.

She finally met her end in a freak accident. Laid up in a shed during World War II, the once-proud *America* was crushed to splinters in 1942, when a heavy load of spring snow collapsed the shed roof.

Stevens tried to pay for the repairs, the hospitable Royal Navy refused.

There was also some attempt at rationalization in the Solent shipyards, including the argument that *America* was a radical racing machine, "a mere shell, a Yankee trick." One shipbuilder told Stevens flatly: "We will build a boat in ninety days that will beat the *America* for £500" (about $2,500). Stevens politely replied, "We'd like to accommodate you, but $2,500 won't pay us for waiting ninety days—not by any means. Make it £25,000 and we'll stay and sail the race." The shipbuilder declined.

The torn copper shoe on her keel repaired in dry dock, *America* was ready for her £100 match race against *Titania*. The latter yacht had been entered in the squadron's round-the-island regatta but had been withdrawn, perhaps in anticipation of the more conclusive test on August 28. It was conclusive: In a strong wind that whipped up to an afternoon gale, *America* led *Titania* on a 40-mile course from the Nab out into the Channel and back, winning by nearly an hour despite a delay to repair her main gaff.

Still, Commodore Stevens and the other syndicate members had reason to feel disappointed. Their yacht had won what appeared to be fleeting glory and only £100 in cash. There was little prospect of further wagers in Britain, and even less at home. Moreover, it was the end of August and the height of the hurricane season on the Atlantic. But to put up the yacht for the winter in England would have been expensive. So the members decided to sell her.

Lord John de Blaquière, a wealthy Irishman who had served in the Army in India, had offered £5,000 for *America*, just enough to make it possible for her owners to declare a modest profit. At the exchange rate of five dollars per pound sterling, the syndicate would realize $5,000 more than the yacht's original $20,000 cost. Add £100 won in the match against *Titania*, subtract £750 that they calculated as their expenses for the trip to England, and the syndicate came out £350, or $1,750, in the black, without counting the value of the Hundred Guinea Cup. So Stevens and his afterguard, including Dick Brown, drank a last toast to their handsome yacht in her spacious cockpit. And *America* was turned over to John de Blaquière.

A few days later Commodore Stevens, accompanied by his brother and Colonel and Mrs. Hamilton, cradled the big, ornate pitcher in his arm as he walked up the gangplank of a steamer for New York. British yacht designers meanwhile were eagerly studying the lines of the sharp bow and slim hull of the yacht *America*, and already there was some muttering about avenging so humiliating a defeat.

As for Stevens, even after returning triumphant to a proud and clamorous New York, he still had not the slightest premonition of the historic feats of yacht racing that *America* would precipitate. At the time, in fact, he was much more concerned over another matter: On his arrival home, his wife, Maria, asked if he had found his prized 50-year-old Madeira. Without remembering to tell her husband, she had stowed it in a secret locker and, indeed, neither Stevens nor the thirsty Steers brothers had uncovered it. The wine was still hidden aboard *America* when she was sold to her new owner.

Chapter 3

A trophy that moved men to excellence and anger

n October 1, 1851, a few days after the schooner *America's* crew returned from their surprising triumph over British yachts at the Isle of Wight, the New York Yacht Club threw a lavish party at the opulent Astor House hotel to celebrate the achievement. As the climax of an elaborate 10-course banquet, waiters bore in a parade of ornamental desserts. One was a faithful reproduction—in flour, butter and candies—of the New York Yacht Club's clubhouse. Another, even more elaborate, was a spun-sugar re-creation of *America* herself, under a full racing rig, leaving a rival in her wake.

About midnight, Commodore John Cox Stevens, as the leader of the six-man syndicate that had built and raced *America*, unveiled the silver trophy he had brought back from England, the Royal Yacht Squadron's Hundred Guinea Cup. All assembled were suitably awed by the achievement it represented—the besting of 14 of Britain's fleetest racing yachts—but some were also struck by the curious, even grotesque, appearance of the trophy itself. Though called a cup, the object—more than two feet high—closely resembled an oversized pitcher, or ewer, and even by Victorian standards it was exuberantly ornate—a veritable riot of bulges, curlicues, scrolls and shields. Its bulging midriff bore not only the legend that *America* had won it, but also a list of the yachts she had beaten in the famous race (unaccountably, *Aurora*, the trim little cutter that had almost caught her, was omitted).

After the banquet, the trophy, which was the joint property of all six syndicate members, was put on display in the parlor of Stevens' Washington Square mansion. Other members borrowed it for ceremonial occasions and showed it off during their own banquets and balls. In 1855 Stevens' wife, Maria, died and the commodore decided to retire to his country estate near South Amboy, New Jersey. When his city house was being closed, the unlovely ewer, which had been banished to a closet and now lay darkly tarnished, was almost relegated to the rubbish wagon. It was saved by Stevens' sharp-eyed butler, who spied it as it was being taken out and gave it to one of Stevens' friends for safekeeping.

For a time the syndicate members who remained in New York debated what to do with the cup. Someone suggested that they have it melted down to make souvenir medals for the members' grandchildren. But in the end they decided to present it to the New York Yacht Club as a permanent challenge trophy. They drew up a paper to that effect and sent it to New Jersey for Stevens' imprimatur. He signed it, but he was fatally ill at the time, and his attendants did not return the paper until

Stylish spectators view an America's Cup race off New York from the canopied afterdeck of a steam yacht in this engraving from an 1886 Harper's Weekly. Less well-off enthusiasts watched from public excursion steamers (center background)—if they could get tickets. New York ships were booked so fast, Harper's noted, that "Boston had to be drawn upon to satisfy the demand."

July 8, 1857, a month after his death. The New York members promptly put this date on the document, signed it themselves and sent it on to the club along with the trophy.

The paper, technically a deed of gift to the New York Yacht Club, was to become the most famous and, because of the way it was worded, the most controversial document in the history of yacht racing. It would change the very structure of yachting competition. Nearly all races up to this time had been restricted to members of a single yacht club, with occasional interclub regattas. The cup itself had been won by *America* on an impromptu basis, through an invitation from the Royal Yacht Squadron to the visiting American schooner. Now the syndicate's deed of gift made yacht racing an international sport: It invited not only the British but all foreign yachtsmen to challenge the New York Yacht Club for the cup. Under the document's terms, the New York Yacht Club would have the authority to accept or refuse any challenge and to set the rules for the match. But, most important, the deed called for any challenger to duplicate the feat of *America*—that is, to sail across the ocean and compete in a regatta with a number of American yachts.

The America's Cup, as it would later be officially designated, would become the focus of intense rivalry. It would attract international public attention to the glamorous world of the yachtsman and kindle widespread speculation in sporting journals as to the merits and disadvantages of particular captains, boats and hull configurations. Naval architects around the world would be pressed to design ever-faster boats to vie for the homely—but coveted—symbol of excellence, and over the years crews contending for it would be recruited more and more selectively and would be trained with increasing sophistication. Fortunes would be spent in the quest for the Cup. But the same powerful lure of the trophy that would spark these efforts to sporting excellence also, at times, would engender such bitterness and controversy that there would be some yachtsmen who would wish Commodore Stevens' butler had never saved the Cup from the trash heap.

The world of yachtsmen is one in which such titles as "gentleman" and "sportsman" are taken seriously. But it is also one of fiercely competitive individuals. Occasionally, when honor and victory seemed to be mutually exclusive goals, some contenders chose the latter. Defenders of the Cup often drew such tight restrictions into the rules that they hampered a fair challenge. Aching under the restrictions, challengers cunningly negotiated to change them, and often loudly protested the rules when they lost. And each time there was a disagreement or an argument or a claim of foul, both sides would turn to the deed of gift to look for language that might justify their positions.

Upon accepting the syndicate's deed of gift, the New York Yacht Club duly informed foreign yachtsmen that the lists were open and that challenges for the Cup would be entertained. The official notification reached the Royal Yacht Squadron—thought by most people to be the most likely challenger—on the Isle of Wight late in 1857.

At first there was no response. While some members still grumped a bit about the upstart Americans' victory six years earlier, none had seriously considered a formal attempt to retrieve the trophy. There were plenty of cups to compete for in Britain, and most members were busy—as a result of *America's* performance—building and fitting out new boats that copied her sleek lines and flat sails. To be sure, these sharp-bowed derivatives of *America* were clearly demonstrating their superiority, not only over their British predecessors but also over the few American visitors that appeared from time to time off England's shores.

Even *America* herself, under her new Irish owner, lost some races to the new British boats. One yacht that beat her, in fact, was *Arrow*, which had run aground in the 1851 race and had been newly rebuilt along *America's* slimmer lines. Yet another loser in the 1851 race, *Alarm*, modified and suited with more tightly woven cotton sails, also outsailed *America* on the Solent. Still, there was no rush to respond to the New York Yacht Club's invitation. And in 1861 the outbreak of the Civil War in the United States and the initiation of Britain's naval effort to aid the Confederacy postponed any thought of Anglo-American yacht racing.

Not until some years after the War did the idea resurface. In 1868 British yachtsmen were agog over the arrival of an American yacht named *Sappho*. With her huge hull and long water line, she looked to be another wonder from the New World. In keeping with sporting tradition, the Royal Yacht Squadron invited her to enter the annual regatta around the Isle of Wight that summer. Surprisingly, she came in fifth, and the taste of revenge began to tempt a few British yachtsmen. Not least tempted was the man whose yacht had won the 1868 Isle of Wight race.

James Ashbury, owner of the schooner *Cambria*, was an Englishman of leisure. The son of a wheelwright who had made a fortune by inventing a modern railway carriage, Ashbury devoted a large part of his time to yachting. The rest of it, evidently, he spent corresponding with the New York Yacht Club. His first challenge was a complicated proposal for a contest on both sides of the Atlantic. He asked that the New York club send a yacht of its choice to compete in two of the 1869 British regattas for one-hundred-pound cups, race *Cambria* back across the Atlantic for a prize of £250, then engage in a two-boat, three-race match around Long Island for the America's Cup.

The New York Yacht Club rejected the challenge, pointing out that the Cup's deed of gift allowed challenges only from recognized yacht clubs, not from individuals. More letters went back and forth across the Atlantic. Ashbury agreed to challenge through the Royal Thames Yacht Club. The New York Yacht Club then reminded him that he had to sail against a fleet of defenders, as *America* had done in 1851. Ashbury blustered. New York was firm. The racing season of 1869 went by.

Early in the 1870 season *Sappho* returned to England. Recently rebuilt, even wider abeam and carrying more canvas, she again raced *Cambria* and this time beat her. But Ashbury was not deterred. Also in English waters that summer was *Dauntless*, a big, fast schooner owned by James Gordon Bennett, publisher of *The New York Tribune*. Ashbury challenged Bennett to a transatlantic race. Bennett accepted. Again Ashbury wrote the New York Yacht Club, proposing to race for the America's Cup when he reached New York. This time he indicated willingness to race against a fleet of Americans, and the club accepted his challenge.

The English *Cambria* and the American *Dauntless* set out across the Atlantic on July 4. Most yachtsmen figured *Dauntless* to be the faster boat, and she had the advantage of having already crossed the Atlantic; any of her gear that had proved unequal to tough, open-ocean conditions had been replaced with sturdier stuff, and her crew was practiced in the challenges of a long crossing. Also, her complement included the New World's best: *America's* skipper in the 1851 Cowes race, Richard "Old Dick" Brown; a renowned Sandy Hook pilot named Martin Lyons; and the redoubtable Sam Samuels, famous as an Atlantic packet skipper.

Even so talented a crew was no proof against mistakes, however. *Dauntless* strayed a few miles off course because of a navigational error, then lost hours searching unsuccessfully for two men swept from her jib boom in midocean. *Cambria* reached Sandy Hook first, by 1 hour 43 minutes, after 23 days of racing. American yachtsmen began to wonder if they would lose their Cup in the first defense.

In 1870 yacht racing in the United States, as in England, was to a great extent a pastime of the wealthy; nonetheless it attracted many spectators. The first challenge for the America's Cup stimulated enormous interest. In New York on August 8, the day of the race, businesses closed down. The harbor swarmed with spectator craft of every size, many festooned with ribbons and pennants. The sailing weather was excellent—sunny skies and a fresh southwesterly breeze. Shortly before 11:30 a.m., 15 defenders arrived at the starting line. One of them was 19-year-old *America* herself. During the Civil War she had been bought by the Confederate Navy *(pages 54-55)*, and now she was a training ship for the United States Navy. Her skipper was Dick Brown, son of Old Dick who had helped bring *Dauntless* across the Atlantic.

The start, as at Cowes 19 years earlier, was from anchor. As a gesture of hospitality, the committee gave *Cambria* the favored position at the windward end of the line. Then, just before the start, the wind shifted. A steward asked Ashbury if he would like to shift position, but Ashbury graciously declined. The starting cannon fired and *Cambria* weighed anchor to avenge England's defeat.

She made a good start, but Franklin Osgood's 13-year-old schooner *Magic*—even quicker off the mark—set the pace for the first leg of the course, which was through the Narrows separating Long Island and Staten Island. *America*, anchored alongside *Cambria* at the start, got away last, just as she had off Cowes.

The New York Yacht Club's inside course, so named because most of it was sailed inside the confines of New York Harbor, was nearly as tricky as the course around the Isle of Wight. There were not so many dangerous shoals, but there were shallows aplenty, strong tides and swift currents. There also seemed to be even more spectator craft than in the Solent, and the American Sunday-afternoon skippers were unaccustomed to maneuvering around a racing fleet. With understandable curiosity, the onlookers crowded the challenger. Ashbury's skipper managed to keep clear of them as he ran through the Narrows and into the Lower Bay. But most of the defenders, taking advantage of their knowledge of the local tides and currents, were passing *Cambria*; at the first mark, Southwest Spit off Sandy Hook, she was in 12th place. On the next leg, however, she began to foot well and to work her way back through the fleet. Then, after rounding the next mark, Sandy Hook Lightship, her captain made a mistake.

Evidently aiming for plenty of sea room, perhaps because of the many contestants and the large spectator fleet, *Cambria's* skipper looped wide over toward Coney Island, into an area of innumerable hidden shallows and swirling currents. The English boat got caught in a current, and while *Magic* increased her lead, *Cambria* was swept off course. Then, to add to her troubles, she was crowded by another contestant, *Tarolinta*. Jibing around to get clear and head back for the finish line, *Cambria* was rocked sharply by an unexpected puff of wind. Her fore-topmast cracked and bent away. She slowed in the water as crewmen hastily lowered her topsail, and most of the American yachts passed her. *Magic's* skipper, who had ridden a gentle ebb tide along the New Jersey shore and had rounded the lightship neatly, laid a straight, short course for home to win the race. *America*, her former speed inhibited by age, a slower rig and Navy midshipmen who were no match for racing yachtsmen, came in fourth. Challenger *Cambria* finished tenth.

Ashore, there was considerable sentiment that *Tarolinta* had committed a foul by crowding *Cambria* off Coney Island. Ashbury either did not think so or, more accurately perhaps, figured that a protest would not be upheld; he did not file one. Taking his defeat with good grace, he re-

Passing the Sandy Hook Lightship, the British yacht Cambria arrives under full sail from the British Isles on July 27, 1870. As the first challenger for the America's Cup, Cambria was to race against a fleet of 15 American yachts in New York Bay 12 days later.

mained in the United States for the rest of the summer, racing in other regattas and winning a few. He enjoyed the hospitality of New York's high society, gave parties of his own and once entertained President Ulysses S. Grant at breakfast aboard *Cambria*. On his return to England, however, the disappointed challenger found himself in the middle of public mutterings about the possible foul. He believed that it was in his interest to play down any bad feeling—he had decided to challenge again—but his yachting compatriots were less willing than he to let the matter drop. The America's Cup thus became a subject of backbiting and ill will with the very first challenge. And the Anglo-American yacht-racing relationship would get worse before it got better.

In making his second challenge in 1871, Ashbury first set out to change the rules of the game, which he regarded as unfair. Opening another barrage of correspondence with the New York Yacht Club, he proposed that the Cup be defended by one yacht against one challenger.

The members in New York were in a quandary. Some saw reason in Ashbury's argument, but others contended that the club was bound by the deed of gift to require any challenger to accomplish what *America* had in winning the Cup: sail across the Atlantic and defeat a fleet of yachts. To resolve the dispute the club turned to the last surviving signer of the deed, George L. Schuyler.

Schuyler, a fair-minded man who over the years would be hailed as a voice of moderation and restraint in Cup negotiations, studied the deed and gave a Solomon-like judgment, one that basically upheld Ashbury's position but still assuaged the feelings of club members who believed the document was sacrosanct. Seizing on an important word in the deed—"match"—he noted that a match is generally regarded as a contest between two yachts. Anything else could be called a "sweepstakes or a regatta," he wrote. "The present ruling of the club renders *America's* trophy useless as a challenge cup, and for all sporting purposes it might as well be laid aside as family plate."

In response, the club made the first important move to relax the rules, informing Ashbury that his challenger would be met by only one defender. But at the same time, the club members could not resist writing in a loophole to help ensure victory. The single defender would be selected on the morning of the race from among four nominees. This ruling served the Americans' purpose nearly as well as having multiple defenders; on a windy race day, a heavy-weather defender could be selected; if the breezes were gentle, a light-weather boat would meet the challenger. But there would be only one challenger, a yacht sturdy enough to sail across the Atlantic.

Manifestly unfair, responded Ashbury. But America's Cup fever had infected him, as it would so many others over the years. He argued for more compromises: seven out of 12 races instead of one sudden-death contest, and a course outside New York Harbor, where his transatlantic challenger might find windier, more favorable conditions.

While the letters went back and forth, Ashbury built his new yacht, *Livonia*. She was bigger than *Cambria*—127 feet long overall, with a reported sail area of more than 18,000 square feet. By the time she was

Winter thrills for icebound yachtsmen

A party of ice yachters streaks along the frozen Hudson River, one member riding as ballast on the starboard cross brace.

The yachting mania of the 19th Century was not confined to the summer season. Driven from the sea by winter gales, a diehard core of American yachtsmen simply moved inland to skim across frozen lakes and rivers in craft like the one above, pictured in *Harper's Weekly* in 1879. A ride in an ice yacht could be frigid, bumpy and loud, as the steel-shod runners chattered across ridges in the ice. But it offered the irresistible thrill of pure speed. With a clear surface and a strong wind abeam, a crack ice yacht might travel at 60 mph or more, twice as fast as the swiftest clipper ship.

The first iceboats, launched on the Hudson River near the beginning of the 19th Century, were comparatively sluggish creations consisting of little more than oblong boxes fitted with runners and spritsails. But over the years the design improved. The hull became a latticework frame of wire and timber, with a crosspiece amidships to hold a pair of runners, a third runner aft to serve as a rudder, and the whole surmounted by a sweep of jib and gaff-rigged mainsail. Seagoing yachtsmen found the craft awkward and skit-

tery, given to sudden pauses, abrupt bursts of acceleration, and an occasional capsize when a windward runner lofted skyward in a gust. But once a sailor got the hang of the sport, there was no stopping him.

Inevitably, speed aroused an urge to race. Poughkeepsie founded an ice-yacht club in 1861. Rival clubs soon sprang up—upstream at Hyde Park, downstream at Newburgh, and on the Shrewsbury River in New Jersey. Throughout the winter, members of all these clubs defied snow squalls and chill winds to vie for cups and pennants.

Competition was usually divided into classes according to sail area; the racers ranged from "mosquito boats" with 150 square feet of canvas to giants such as John Roosevelt's *Icicle,* 69 feet long and carrying 1,070 square feet of sail. When no races were scheduled on the Hudson, skippers sometimes tested their boats against the express locomotives of Commodore Vanderbilt's New York Central Railroad, which ran along the river. The ice yachts usually won. They "didn't sail," said an enthusiast, "they flew."

launched the summer months of 1871 were fleeting, so Ashbury took a chance and brought her to the United States while he and the New York Yacht Club continued to bicker. It was October 1 when *Livonia* docked, and the talks were still going on. "It's becoming cold," Ashbury finally said. "Let's get it over with." He settled for four out of seven races, alternating between the inside course and another that would take the contestants 20 miles into the open ocean from Sandy Hook Lightship and return. The club was permitted to put up a different defender for each race, if it so chose, and it did not need to announce its choice until the morning of that race.

Despite the lateness of the season, there was but little wind on October 16, the day of the first race. The New York Yacht Club's strategy of multiple choice paid off. *Columbia*, a centerboard schooner owned by Franklin Osgood, whose *Magic* had beaten Ashbury's first challenger, made the most of the light breezes and won easily over the inside course. But in the next race, on the outside course two days later, the club's selection strategy backfired.

The day started with gentle breezes and the defenders chose *Columbia* again. But an hour after the cannon had boomed, the breezes freshened to near-gale force. *Columbia* buried her rail and then her lee deck, sloshing tons of water to both sides as she wallowed through churning seas. *Livonia*, crowding on sail, moved ahead and held a commanding lead at the outer mark. Then occurred a maddening incident reminiscent of *America's* race around the Isle of Wight 20 years earlier.

The course instructions, given to both skippers before the race, specified rounding a boat staked 20 miles to windward of the starting line. Unfortunately, as in the race around the Isle of Wight two decades before, the instructions were silent on whether to leave this mark to port or starboard. *Columbia's* captain had queried the men on the committee boat about this and had been assured that the mark could be rounded either way. But no one in the committee boat had thought to mention the ambiguity to Ashbury's captain, who was accustomed to leaving all marks to starboard, as was common practice in England.

Thus *Livonia's* skipper, having set an enormous press of sail for the downwind outward run, jibed around the mark, leaving it to starboard. This jibe was a tricky maneuver, if not downright dangerous, with a full spread of canvas; by the time the sheets could be hauled in close for the beat home, *Livonia* was well off course. The captain of *Columbia*, meanwhile, opted for a much simpler and less time-consuming turn. He sailed past the mark to leeward, luffed up through the wind rather than jibing, and left the stake boat to port. His sails fell neatly onto the other tack and he set out for home, on course and in the lead. *Livonia* never caught up.

Ashbury promptly protested, demanding at least that the second race be rerun. The New York Yacht Club refused. Its rules did not require rounding the mark as *Livonia* had done, and that was that. Ashbury sputtered, but the committee held firm.

So far it had been a two-boat match, *Livonia* versus *Columbia*. For the third race, however, the committee selected *Dauntless*, the schooner that Ashbury's old *Cambria* had narrowly beaten across the Atlantic the

Wearing natty spats and holding his yachting telescope, rail-car heir James Ashbury lounges in the cockpit of Livonia, the 127-foot schooner in which he made his second try for the coveted America's Cup in 1871. Ashbury, who held memberships in a dozen yacht clubs, aspired to represent all of them in 12 separate contests for the Cup.

previous year. The crewmen of *Columbia*, looking forward to a day's rest, over-celebrated their two victories. They were startled the next morning to discover that *Dauntless* had lost part of her bowsprit in a towing accident, and that *Columbia* would again defend. But many of her crewmen were simply too hung over to function. Even the skipper was incapacitated, though by an injury to his hand, not a hang-over. The mix-up was the break Ashbury needed. *Columbia*, manned largely by hastily recruited sailors and a substitute skipper who was unfamiliar with her rig, plodded around the course, and *Livonia* romped home ahead of her by 19 minutes.

For the fourth race the committee selected *Sappho*, and in a wild, windy contest, with seas rushing the length of their decks, she beat *Livonia* to the finish line. Two days later she did it again.

Ashbury's *Livonia* had now been defeated in four of five races. By the reckoning of the New York Yacht Club, the America's Cup had again been successfully defended.

Ashbury, however, disagreed. He reminded the committee of the protested second race and, apparently withdrawing his offer to resail it, claimed it as a victory. Since *Livonia* had won the third contest, Ashbury figured that the series stood at three for the defenders to two for him. He would, he said, be at sea the next day to sail race No. 6, and the following day for race No. 7. If the New York Yacht Club chose not to meet him with a defender, he would claim those two races—and thus the series—by default.

True to his word, he took *Livonia* out next morning. *Dauntless*, too, was at sea, and her captain said he would be glad to sail an informal race. But, he added, in the view of the club the series had been completed. They raced, and *Livonia* lost. Still Ashbury counted the contest in his own victory column. To anyone who would listen he argued that since *Dauntless* had not been officially posted by the committee as the day's defender, the race was his by default.

The next day both *Livonia* and *Dauntless* appeared at the starting line again, but the wind was so strong and the seas so steep that no one would take a stake boat out to serve as a mark. Again Ashbury claimed a default. By his reckoning, he had now won four races—one by protest, one on the course and two by default. He formally requested that the New York Yacht Club hand over the America's Cup. The club refused. Ashbury returned to England, complaining to the press about the Americans' "unsportsmanlike proceedings." British journals huffed at what they considered Yankee cunning.

Finally, as the vituperation swelled to a crescendo, the New York Yacht Club felt called upon to issue a protest of its own. And it did so in terms that could hardly have been better calculated to arouse the ire of British yachtsmen. "There are certain acts which a gentleman cannot commit," the New Yorkers sniffed in a cable to a group of Ashbury's supporters. Then to end the exchange they returned three cups that Ashbury had donated to them as race prizes.

Still, Ashbury's contentiousness induced the Americans to make yet another change in the rules. The New York Yacht Club, which had been berated by Americans as well as Englishmen for the unfairness of switching yachts in mid-series, decided that for future challenges it would select only a single defender. Even so, the New Yorkers, dismayed by the rancor and ill will that had resulted from the races with Ashbury, resigned themselves to waiting a long time for another challenge. The wait did last a full five years, and then in 1876 the members were startled to receive an offer from an unexpected quarter.

The bid came from the Royal Canadian Yacht Club, one of whose members, a Captain Alexander Cuthbert, was designing and building a fishing schooner that he thought fast enough to run for the Cup. Pitting a fishing boat against the pampered yachts of the wealthy was not so peculiar a proposal as it would seem today. Such working boats in the late 19th Century were famous for their seaworthiness and speed. They were designed to race one another from offshore fishing grounds to market, where the first arrivals got the highest prices.

Some New Yorkers, however, had misgivings of another sort about the challenge. The Canadian club, after all, was not even located on an ocean; it was in Toronto on Lake Ontario. The New Yorkers, with a prejudice common among salt-water sailors, wondered how a fresh-water yachtsman could hope to give them a run for their money. But a challenge from Toronto was better than no challenge at all, and the New Yorkers accepted the bid. Later, they would regret their decision—though not for any reason they might have anticipated.

The Canadian challenger, which was grandly named *Countess of Dufferin*, cost more to build than Cuthbert and his syndicate of co-owners could afford. A hasty appeal among other Canadian yachtsmen brought in enough money to complete her, but on her arrival in New York she looked to local yachtsmen like a poor Midwestern copy of a Yankee fisherman. Her sails, one reporter wrote, were "set like a purser's shirt on a handspike," and her hull was "rough as a nutmeg grater." Overall, she appeared to be clearly outclassed by the chosen defender, a graceful and well-appointed sloop named *Madeleine.*

Countess was badly beaten in the first of the agreed-upon three races. Captain Cuthbert, who had taken the helm himself instead of hiring a professional skipper as was the general custom in Cup competition, enlisted a local pilot for the second contest. *Countess* nonetheless lost again. Then the New York Yacht Club, whose dignity had already suffered from having accepted a challenge that proved so nearly a sail-over, suffered an even greater embarrassment: A sheriff came to attach *Countess* to pay off her owners' outstanding debts. The ignominy was compounded a few nights later when Cuthbert crept aboard the schooner and spirited her away from the sheriff. The New York Yacht Club members shuddered at the bad publicity.

They shuddered again four years later when Cuthbert sent a second challenge, this time through the Bay of Quinte Club in Belleville, Ontario. But with no other prospects on the horizon, the New York yachtsmen reluctantly accepted. Cuthbert's new challenger, *Atalanta,* was brought to New York by barge on the Erie Canal, heeled over to fit through the narrow locks and dragged along by mules. While the New York Yacht Club members winced at the hilarity with which yachting writers reported on the mule-powered challenger's progress, the committee chose the sloop *Mischief* to defend. In two races, sailed in strong winds, she easily disposed of *Atalanta.* In the second race, the Canadian sailed so badly that the race committee ordered a tugboat to stay near her in case she capsized. *The Spirit of the Times,* a New York journal, contemptuously called *Atalanta* "hastily built and miserably equipped," and pronounced the entire episode "a stupid comedy." The America's Cup as a yacht-racing institution had become a mockery.

The members of the New York Yacht Club began to question why they had accepted the trophy in the first place, for now Cuthbert was threatening to lay up his yacht in New York for the winter and continue the farce with an 1882 challenge. Some members proposed that the competition be permanently ended. Others, however, felt that the true difficulty lay not in the rancorous disputes with the British or in the eccentricities of the Canadians, but in the document that set the basic conditions for the races. What was needed was a new deed of gift. After an anguished meeting, the club returned the Cup to George Schuyler and asked him to compose a new deed of gift that would rescue the dignity of the competition. He promptly complied.

Hereafter, Schuyler proposed, no challenge would be accepted from a club that did not customarily hold its regattas on salt water (that took care of the Great Lakes Canadians). The challenger must sail to New York on the open ocean. And no vessel that had been defeated could challenge again in less than two years, unless there had been an intervening match. With the rules thus altered to meet changing conditions, Schuyler gave the Cup back to the club, just in time for a new challenge.

In the 14 years since the Ashbury contretemps, British tempers had cooled. Now another Briton was succumbing to America's Cup fever. He was Sir Richard Sutton, a genial gentleman who had many American friends. And not only did Sutton open negotiations for his own challenge, he also put forward a subsequent contender, a popular British yachtsman named Lieutenant William Henn who had recently married an heiress and retired from the Royal Navy.

This double offer raised spirits—and glasses—in the bar of the New York Yacht Club. Here was a chance to redeem the prestige of the America's Cup races against worthy competition. Both challenges were quickly accepted. The Sutton challenge would be met in 1885, Henn's in 1886.

"Mohawk's" tragic end: the high price of hubris

She was the queen of New York's racing fleet in 1875, the largest competitive yacht on American waters. Her owner, a 35-year-old textile magnate named William Garner, had set out to build the ultimate in racing schooners, and Mohawk seemed to be just that.

Wide-bellied and flat-bottomed, she carried more than 20,000 square feet of canvas and measured 140 feet overall, with her extraordinary 30-foot beam and a draft of only six feet with her centerboard up. These features made Mohawk tricky at the helm, but lightning fast downwind. She performed well during one season of competition: One season was all she had.

On the afternoon of Thursday, July 20, 1876, the schooner lay anchored at Stapleton, Staten Island. The weather was cloudy with occasional showers, but Mohawk's owner intended to take her out for a sail. He arrived in mid-afternoon with Mrs. Garner and five guests, who shortly went below on the appearance of a sudden shower. In the meantime, the crew hoisted the schooner's sails and made the sheets fast in preparation for getting under way.

At about 4:15 the captain, Oliver Rowland, ordered the anchor raised. But the crew had no sooner begun to hoist than a sudden gust of wind tore across the harbor, hit Mohawk's topsails and tipped her violently to port.

"Let go the topsail halyards!" Rowland yelled in alarm. "There's no danger, it's all right," Garner called back. Indeed, the gust passed and the schooner began to right herself.

Suddenly a stronger gust hit. Mohawk was knocked flat. Held down and pushed along by the force of the wind, she rode up on her anchor and literally sailed under the waves. As her fate became clear, Garner rushed below to look for his wife.

The cabin, fast filling with water, was a chaos of tumbled furniture. Mrs. Garner was trapped. A quantity of 150-pound lead ingots, carried as ballast in the hull below the cabin, had smashed through the deck and slipped down to the port side on top of her. "For God's sake, help me pull her out," Garner cried—but it was no use. Moreover, the dislocated ballast made it impossible for the yacht to right herself.

As water cascaded into the cabin, two guests managed to escape up the companionway, and one was able to swim out through a smashed skylight. The rest sank with Mohawk in less than 10 minutes. Five people died in the tragedy: Garner and his wife, two of their friends, and a cabin boy.

The disaster was a tragic compound of accident and misjudgment. An exacting skipper would have left the sheets slack, allowing the wind to spill harmlessly from the sails. At a coroner's inquest Captain Rowland was found innocent of any wrongdoing, but yachtsmen almost universally condemned him for gross negligence.

But they also blamed Mohawk's design, contending that her broad beam and shallow draft—and her dependence on unsecured internal ballast for stability—made her inherently unseaworthy. With Mohawk's capsizing, the fashion for shallow-draft schooners waned, making way for a breed of lean, deep-draft racing yachts.

The twin challenges ushered in a welcome new era for the races, for the New York Yacht Club and for the development of racing yachts. Sutton's *Genesta* represented a new generation of British cutters that had been developing since the 1860s. She boasted a long water line and a deep, heavy keel, which enabled her to carry an enormous spread of canvas. The British term for the new design was "plank-on-edge."

American yachtsmen, too, had been tending away from schooners like *America*, some of which had been built so wide-bodied, shallow-keeled and heavily sparred as to be dangerously unstable in gusty breezes. In one famous tragedy, a huge schooner named *Mohawk*, caught by a sudden gust while at anchor with her sails close-hauled *(pages 72-73)*, capsized and sank in minutes, drowning five people. The accident was blamed at least partly on her unstable design. Now naval architects were designing yachts along the new, more seaworthy lines, and the Sutton challenge sparked a vigorous competition to come up with an American boat fast enough to defend the Cup.

From Boston came reports of a syndicate that was willing to bankroll

Caught by a squall, Mohawk begins to capsize. Though not shown in this newspaper engraving, her topsails were set when she sank.

an effort. The New Yorkers smiled indulgently. The designer for the
Boston syndicate was a scarcely known young man named Edward Burgess who, as one New York designer remarked disdainfully, "had no
interest in mathematics or mechanics, and he lacked the technical training considered essential today."

New York club members meanwhile turned to the famous South Street
naval architect A. Cary Smith, who employed all the latest concepts and
already had proved himself with the 1881 defender, *Mischief.* Smith's
nominee, named *Priscilla,* was almost an exact copy of Sutton's challenger, *Genesta:* 96½ feet long overall, narrow in beam and deep in draft.
But Edward Burgess' creation, named *Puritan,* was something even
newer. Under her 94-foot hull was a keel only 8½ feet deep but all of 51
feet long, plus a centerboard that slipped up inside the keel and could be
lowered to increase her draft to 20 feet. She went like the wind. Burgess'
Puritan, earlier derided as the "Boston bean boat," easily won two of
three trial races against Smith's *Priscilla* and was selected as defender.

The morning of the first race, September 8, 1885, was a beautiful one
for racing, breezy, with a wind from the southeast. The day would be

*Her bowsprit splintered in a prestart
collision in 1885, Britain's Genesta begins
to make repairs while the New York
Yacht Club committee boat approaches to
offer her the race on the ground that
she had been fouled. Genesta's owner, Sir
Richard Sutton, sportingly refused and
volunteered to race again. He lost, but won
widespread American good will.*

marred, however, by a mishap that, paradoxically, did much to restore good feelings to the America's Cup matches. With only two yachts competing in a match race, the rules now called for a running start instead of a start from anchor. As *Genesta* and *Puritan* maneuvered at the two-minute warning gun, *Genesta* was on the starboard tack, *Puritan* on the port tack. Rapidly the distance between them decreased. *Puritan's* captain knew he did not have the right of way but—playing a game of bluff and counterbluff that was common in yacht racing—he refused to yield, hoping *Genesta's* skipper would give way and thus allow *Puritan* a better position at the starting line. The latter was not cowed and held his course. *Puritan's* helm was put over too late, her mainsail caught the tip of *Genesta's* bowsprit and snapped it off.

Without even waiting for *Genesta* to hoist her protest flag, the committee disqualified *Puritan*. From the committee boat they hailed Sir Richard: *Genesta* had only to sail the course to be declared winner of the first race. Sutton immediately demurred. "We are obliged to you," he called out, "but we want a race, not a sail-over." The contest was postponed. Nor would Sutton permit the American syndicate to pay for the repairs. Word promptly spread through New York. The America's Cup—and America's Cup challengers—were popular again.

Despite his affability, however, Sutton was no more successful on the racecourse than his predecessors had been. In the first completed 1885 race, *Genesta* lost to *Puritan*; although *Genesta* had been somewhat hampered by the choppy wakes of an overly enthusiastic spectator fleet, Sutton declined to protest. The second race was a thundering thrash offshore in winds gusting to 40 knots. *Genesta's* lofty sails proved too much for her, burying her lee rail in the surging seas. She lost by two minutes. At the end of the race, and the series, the British crew saluted the winner with three cheers, which were heartily answered by the Americans. America's Cup harmony had been restored.

The following year Lieutenant Henn proved nearly as popular, but for a different reason. Since his retirement from the Royal Navy, Henn had spent most of his time aboard his yacht *Galatea*, whose luxurious appointments included draperies, leopard-skin rugs and potted plants. In the summer of 1886 American yachtsmen greeted the *Galatea* with mild consternation when they found the lieutenant and his wife aboard with a retinue of dogs and a pet monkey. The plants were put ashore for the contest, but Mrs. Henn and the animals remained aboard, discreetly keeping below while *Galatea* lost the first two out of three races to another Burgess-designed defender, *Mayflower*.

The next challengers, a Scottish syndicate from the Royal Clyde Yacht Club, added to the climate of good will by arriving in 1887 with a band of bagpipers and cases of their popular national beverage. Speculation about the race ran higher than usual because the syndicate took pains to keep the exact design of their yacht, *Thistle*, a secret. One enterprising New York newspaper editor sent a diver in the dead of night to inspect her underwater lines, which he proudly reproduced in a drawing. But such journalistic derring-do did not bother the syndicate members; one of them merely commented that the reporter might well fear for his job when the boat's true lines were revealed in dry dock after the race.

WILLIAM HENN   MRS. HENN

In the event, *Thistle* proceeded to lose gracefully to the defender, *Volunteer*. The acrimony of earlier years by now seemed safely past. This was just as well, because the worst dispute of all was yet to come.

Windham Thomas Wyndham-Quin, fourth Earl of Dunraven, was a brilliant, many-talented, handsome, hawk-nosed patrician. Born into the Irish aristocracy, he trained for years to become a concert violinist but ultimately decided that "the sea was the master passion," as he put it in his memoirs. In his long sailing career he owned 14 yachts and wrote authoritative works on naval architecture. He also could be argumentative and arrogant, which might have been one reason why it took three years to negotiate the terms of the challenge that was first proposed for him by the Royal Yacht Squadron in 1889.

Much of the delay, at least in the early stages, was the New York club's fault. In the 1887 Scottish challenge there had been a question about *Thistle's* water-line length. The matter had been settled amicably enough, but to stave off any future questions the club again called on the fair and flexible-minded Schuyler to redraft the deed of gift. This time the club appointed a committee to help him. That there were too many lawyers—amateur and professional—on the committee was indicated by the amount of verbiage it produced. The new deed of gift bristled with whereases and aforesaids, and contained provisions that seemed designed more to govern an international treaty conference than a yacht race. One clause, for instance, required any challenger to announce 10 months before the race the general specifications of his yacht, including exact sail area and water-line length. This would give the Americans an

Opulent clutter, including leopard-skin rugs and fine china, fills the main cabin of Galatea, the 1886 America's Cup challenger, which was owned by William Henn (opposite). Such extravagances were not unusual on the racing yachts of the wealthy, but Henn did have one novelty along: his wife, the first woman to sail in an America's Cup race.

advantage: They would have time to build a defender expressly designed to take on the challenging yacht.

But as a committee composed mostly of yachtsmen should have known, an exact prediction of water-line length was nearly impossible; much depended on ballast alone, for example. Because a boat tapers down to the keel, her water line will be shorter or longer depending on how light or heavy her ballast is. And before a boat is built, one cannot tell how much ballast will be needed to adjust her trim for racing.

British yachtsmen cried foul. England's Yacht Racing Association, representing most of the country's sailing clubs, concluded that "the terms of the new deed of gift are such that foreign vessels are unable to challenge," and the Royal Yacht Squadron withdrew the challenge it had proposed for Lord Dunraven.

Dunraven himself thereupon took over the negotiations. He had once served as a Foreign Office diplomat, and now he applied the skills he had gained in that service in an attempt to modify some of the new deed's restrictions. On the American side, however, the spirit of compromise suffered a blow during the night of July 31, 1890, when George Schuyler died aboard the yacht *Electra* in New York Harbor. It took two more years, until late 1892, before Dunraven finally won an agreement from the New York club, which consented not only to be lenient about the exact water-line length of the challenging yacht, but to extend the series by two races, to the best of five.

Dunraven's challenger was the second of three yachts he named *Valkyrie*. *Valkyrie II* was 87 feet long at the water line, and sleek and slim, with a great press of sail. Her appearance in New York in 1893 attracted crowds, but Dunraven himself, who arrived later by steamer, created even more of a sensation.

The perfect picture of the aristocratic British yachtsman, with his handle-bar mustache, his high, tanned brow, his keen eyes and his impeccable yachting kit, the Earl of Dunraven was an instant success with title-loving New Yorkers. In fact, he recalled later, when the pain of a gout attack caused him "to limp about New York in one brown shoe and one list slipper," the young dandies of Manhattan society immediately turned out wearing one shoe and one carpet slipper as the latest fashion.

Although Dunraven was lionized by New York socialites, the 35-man crew of his yacht greeted him with mixed emotions. Discovering that his men had succumbed to the fleshpots of New York and were suffering from an overindulgence in beef and beer, Dunraven recalled, "I had to put them on a severe diet." The regimen he imposed included a medicinal ration of grog mixed with other ingredients that he called a *Valkyrie* cocktail; though he never divulged the exact formula, it was, he admitted, "a nauseous black-dose prescription, concocted in large cans, and served out daily."

The defenders of the Cup, meanwhile, had prepared their own reception for *Valkyrie II* in the form of a trim cutter named *Vigilant*. Edward Burgess had died of typhoid fever in 1891 and the Americans had turned to Nathanael G. Herreshoff, a man who was already being called the "Wizard of Bristol" for the record-breaking sloops and cutters he was turning out in that seaside Rhode Island town. For the 1893 challenge he came up with a short hull—86 feet at the water line—and then crowded some 2,000 square feet more sail onto her than would normally be carried by a yacht her size. So evenly matched were the challenger and the defender that the ensuing contest was the closest so far in the 23 years of Cup competition.

The series started ominously for the defenders, however. The first race, which was sailed on October 5, was 15 miles out to leeward and return. The wind was light but fickle. As *Valkyrie II* made way on the first leg, her crew succeeded in setting a bleached muslin spinnaker that filled so easily in the light airs that many in the large spectator fleet mistook it for silk. At the mark the challenger was 26 minutes ahead. Then the wind died; with both of the yachts becalmed, the race committee called a halt to the contest.

On October 7 the first race was resailed in winds that were moderate,

In the summer of 1887, workmen at a Boston yard put the finishing touches on Volunteer, which was built in a record 66 days in response to the challenge of the Scottish yacht Thistle. Volunteer's reefing bowsprit, a novel feature, was retractable and could be adjusted in length to suit different wind conditions.

and Herreshoff's design proved itself, with *Vigilant* the winner. On October 9 the second race went off, and *Vigilant* again romped home first.

Two days later the air was practically dead calm at the start of the third race, and both boats had to be towed back in after a long, exasperating drift. The race was rescheduled for October 13, and it would be decisive if *Vigilant* won again.

From the outset it appeared that she would not. On this Friday the 13th the wind was piping out of the east up to 30 knots, and the race was on the outside course, from Sandy Hook Lightship, 15 miles to windward and return. Both captains ordered reefs in their mainsails for the beat out. Still the strong gusts laid both yachts almost over on their sides. Aboard the vessels, little could be heard above the smashing seas and the shrieking of the wind in the shrouds; commands had to be relayed from man to man along the listing decks. Within minutes everyone was soaked through his oilskins.

Vigilant had an extra-large crew of 70 aboard; there was at the time no

In a race full of hard-luck surprises,
a fierce gale bursts the giant spinnaker of
Lord Dunraven's Valkyrie II and sends
the defending Vigilant surging past in the
1893 Cup series. Dunraven, who later
found fault with the American race
organizers, spectators and contestants,
seemed to blame this accident, too, on the
host country. "I have never known it to
happen in England," he said.

regulation that limited the number of men a boat could carry, and her owner believed that the weight of the extra men would help balance the boat in heavy seas. Indeed, Captain William Hansen now ordered nearly all of them to lie along *Vigilant's* high, windward rail. Still, *Valkyrie II* steadily increased her lead and, in a tumult of flogging canvas and rattling blocks, she went pitching around the stake boat. Quickly and expertly her crew loosed her sails to the wind, which was now howling from astern, and she seemed almost to surf along the swelling seas as she raced for the finish line.

Hansen took *Vigilant* thrashing around the mark a full 600 yards—almost a third of a mile—astern of *Valkyrie II*. The challenger was going faster than ever, so fast that the big excursion steamers that had ventured offshore could not keep up with her. Hansen decided on a desperate gamble; he would loose more sail to the following wind than any America's Cup skipper had ever done under such near-gale conditions.

On a big racing yacht of the 19th Century, the paid hands who did the heavy work were nearly as important as an expert skipper. These hands were often called "Norwegian steam" because most of them were Scandinavians who worked as hard as steam engines aboard New Yorkers' yachts all summer and then returned home to spend the winter doing the same aboard fishing boats in the Baltic.

One of these men, secured to a line run through a block on the mast, now worked his way out onto *Vigilant's* long boom to unreef the mainsail. With the yacht rushing downwind and rolling heavily from side to side, the boom dipped to within inches of the snarling waves. Sometimes its tip swatted the top off a high comber. Ducking in the spray, the crewman inched his way from one reefing point to the next, cutting the lines that held the folded bottom of the sail to the boom. The loosened canvas bellied out with thundering reports, and crewmen on deck joined in a tug of war with the gale to haul the huge sail taut. Meanwhile, the foredeck gang set *Vigilant's* spinnaker and, in addition, Hansen called for a balloon-jib topsail, a sort of half-spinnaker set at the top of the mast.

Under this downright dangerous expanse of sail, *Vigilant* surged forward. Her topmast groaned and swayed, but luckily held. As the helmsman fought the wheel to keep her from being swung off course, the boat rolled nearly onto her beam ends on one side, then righted to roll almost onto the other. As she began gaining on the challenger, fortune shifted even more in her favor: *Valkyrie II* was in trouble.

As the English boat had rounded the mark, her captain, William Cranfield, apparently decided against shaking out the reefs in her mainsail, but he did order up his spinnaker. As the huge sail rose, however, it caught briefly on a cleat and was slightly torn. Then, as the sail was sheeted home, the rip raced the length of the sail; another rip started, and another; within seconds the crewmen were hauling down a shower of ribbons. Because *Valkyrie II's* backup spinnaker was of lightweight muslin, it too was quickly ripped to shreds. Cranfield was left with only his balloon jib, and that was simply too little foresail to maintain his margin. *Vigilant* went roaring past and streaked across the finish line two minutes and 13 seconds in the lead.

The *New York Times* called this deciding race "probably the greatest battle of sails ever fought." "A splendid race, nobly sailed," added a visiting British yachtsman. Lord Dunraven accepted defeat with grace, but unlike Sir Richard Sutton, who had muted any complaint regarding the intrusive spectators eight years before, the earl muttered that *Valkyrie II* "was greatly interfered with by excursion steamers." Still, he promised to challenge again, adding, "I do not consider that the merits of the two boats have been determined." Although no one could know it at the time, Dunraven's second challenge would bring unprecedented discord that would come close to ending the America's Cup competition forever.

A tragedy that occurred the following summer no doubt had much to do with Dunraven's later truculence. In July *Valkyrie II* was in the Holy Loch, at Clyde, Scotland, maneuvering for the start of a local race that was being held under what the British called "mudhook rules": Only amateurs could take the helm. Thus Dunraven himself was in command.

The day was drizzly and gusty, with erratic squalls sweeping across the course. Dunraven, heading for the starting line on a starboard tack, noticed a big cutter named *Satanita* bearing down on him at express speed, but, since he had the right of way, he expected *Satanita's* helmsman to bear up in time.

Satanita's helmsman, jockeying for an advantageous position at the starting line, in fact had planned to jibe away from *Valkyrie II* at the last moment. Suddenly, however, he spotted a small spectator boat right in the course of his planned maneuver. Immediately he tried luffing up into the wind, but it was too late. Dunraven watched helplessly as 300 tons of wood and steel thundered into *Valkyrie II* amidships.

Tons of sea water rushed through the huge hole that *Satanita* sliced in *Valkyrie II's* hull. Dunraven and his afterguard jumped into the boats that immediately congregated on the scene. The crew as well managed to scramble to safety except for one man who had been below and whose leg was crushed. He was rescued, but died in a hospital. Meanwhile, Dunraven's beloved yacht sank in minutes with all her gear.

The vivid memory of the Clyde collision long remained with Dunraven, and when he brought himself to challenge again for the Cup in 1895 he requested a change of venue from New York to Marblehead, Massachusetts, where he assumed that there would be fewer spectator craft. The New Yorkers did not deliberate long before refusing to change locations. They had no desire to defend the Cup in unfamiliar waters. Dunraven grumbled but agreed, and readied *Valkyrie III*, a new yacht he was having built in Glasgow.

Valkyrie III arrived in New York on August 19. Unlike the Cowes Week race of 1851, America's Cup races were held under handicap rules, which increased the importance of seamanship and ensured that certain design factors—such as longer hulls or larger expanses of sail—would not preordain the outcome of the contest. Accordingly, on September 6, the day before the first race, both *Valkyrie III* and her American opponent *Defender*—Nat Herreshoff's latest creation—were taken to Erie Basin to have their water lines measured. Dunraven, punctilious about every detail, asked that the measurement committee "take every precaution to ensure that the vessels sail on the measured water-line length."

High and dry in a Brooklyn shipyard, Defender awaits polishing of her bronze bottom just before the 1895 racing season. A lighter metal, aluminum, was used for her topsides and deck framing. The weight thus saved enabled her to carry a heavy load of lead ballast low in her keel in order to enhance her stability.

The members of the committee, however, did not attach great significance to this remark; they followed the normal procedure when they measured the boats but forgot to mark their water lines. The oversight appeared insignificant, even trivial at the time, but there would be painful repercussions from it.

The following day it was apparent that Lord Dunraven's second challenge for the America's Cup had attracted an even greater crowd of onlookers than his first. More than 200 pleasure craft—the largest spectator fleet in the history of the Cup—were swarming about the starting line. The New York Yacht Club had engaged 20 picket boats in an effort to keep the spectators at a distance, but they had little success. Most of the steamer captains had no conception of the amount of open water a big racing yacht needed for maneuvering, and their passengers, after all, had paid for a close look at the contenders. There was only a light breeze, and the chop caused by the spectator fleet set *Valkyrie III* and *Defender* rocking and losing the wind from their sails.

Dunraven's *Valkyrie III* won the start and led for more than an hour. But *Defender*, footing well, steadily pulled closer. Then, about halfway to the mark, *Defender* slid narrowly past *Valkyrie III*'s bow and into the lead. On the homeward leg the wind picked up. *Defender*, proving herself a faster boat in a fresh breeze, crossed the finish line eight minutes ahead of the challenger.

Dunraven, with ominous ire, informed Latham Fish, the member assigned to represent the New York Yacht Club aboard *Valkyrie III*, that he was convinced ballast had been brought aboard *Defender* during the night before the race. The added weight, Dunraven alleged, settled her lower in the water, thus lengthening her water line and increasing her maximum speed. Both yachts, said the Irish peer, should be measured again and their water lines should be marked. But he made it clear that this was a private complaint. Publicly he made a different protest. In a letter to the race committee, Dunraven deplored the harassment by the fleet of spectator vessels.

The race committee recognized the significance of Dunraven's private protest and perhaps appreciated why he had not made it public as he had his other complaint. Intrusion by spectators was an unfortunate circumstance; secretly shifting ballast would be nothing less than fraud. The following morning both yachts were measured once again. *Defender*, a tiny bit lower in the water than in her first measurement, was only ⅛ inch longer at the water line—a difference so slight that it could have had no effect in the race. The committee members breathed a collective sigh of relief and forgot about it.

The spectator problem, however, remained. On September 10 an even larger crowd was out for the second race. So bad was the traffic jam around the starting line that at one point during the pregun maneuvers both yachts were lost from the committee boat's view. Then, when the yachts reappeared, the members gasped as a huge steamer wallowed straight across the path of the contenders. *Valkyrie III* managed to slip past her bow and *Defender* went under her stern.

The racers came down to the line on a converging course, still bobbing about in the wake of the steamer. *Defender*, with the right of way, held course. At the last moment, to avoid a collision, *Valkyrie III* luffed up. But as her 105-foot-long boom swung out wide over the leeward rail, the tip caught momentarily on *Defender*'s weather shrouds. One of *Defender*'s piano-wire-tight stays snapped loose, and her topsail tilted away, taking the topmast with it.

Captain Hank Haff brought his wounded yacht up into the wind while crewmen scurried aloft to rerig the topmast. Within a minute and 15 seconds, so well trained was the crew, a new stay was in place and *Defender* crossed the starting line, her red protest flag already flying. *Valkyrie III*, meanwhile, was charging straight down the first leg of the course as if she had committed no foul at all.

Nursing his weakened top-hamper, Captain Haff nearly caught *Valkyrie III*, finishing two minutes after her. *Defender*'s owner, C. Oliver Iselin, duly filed his protest. Dunraven's explanation was that his *Valkyrie III* had established an overlap—that is, she was far enough ahead of *Defender* to have assumed the right of way. Unfortunately for Dunra-

This ad in the Providence Journal promised a front-row seat and more at the 1895 Cup races. The Frances (the abbreviation "St." stands for "steamer") was one of 200 hired tugs, ferryboats and other excursion vessels that jammed into New York Bay for the series, carrying a grand total of 60,000 spectators.

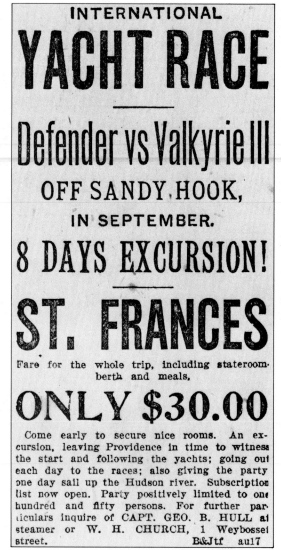

Spectator craft chug airily down the course on race day, blocking the wind and roiling the water for Cup contenders Defender *and* Valkyrie III. *"To race under those conditions is, in my opinion, absurd," complained Lord Dunraven — and many yachtsmen agreed with him.*

ven's defense, photographs had been taken of the incident, and they proved him wrong. Iselin's protest was sustained, and the second race was awarded to *Defender*. Iselin offered to resail the race. Dunraven replied coldly, "I cannot agree. You would not have protested had you not believed that *Valkyrie III* had caused a foul by committing a breach of the rules." He found the committee's reasoning "beyond my comprehension," but its members "have decided that you are right and I am wrong and there the matter ends."

To the committee, however, Dunraven yet again amplified his protest against the fleet of spectator boats. "To attempt to start two such large yachts among moving steamers and tugboats is exceedingly dangerous," the earl complained, and he added that if the race committee was not able to control the spectator fleet, "I will not further risk the lives of my men or the ship."

The waters off Sandy Hook the following day were as crowded as ever. Dunraven brought *Valkyrie III* out to the starting area, but onlookers soon noticed that her racing sails remained below. As the crowd wondered what was wrong, she duly sailed the prerace maneuvers. At the bark of the starting cannon, she sailed across the line and then bore up into the wind. Her racing flag rippled down, to be replaced by the burgee of the New York Yacht Club, which had elected Dunraven to an honorary membership. *Defender* sailed on by herself around the course to win the race by default.

New Yorkers who had lionized the Irish aristocrat, including many who had contributed to the problem by crowding the course, abruptly turned on him and called him a bad loser. The members of the New York Yacht Club were barely civil to him as he and *Valkyrie III* departed for Ireland. Then, two months later, all hell broke loose.

In an article for the *London Field*, Dunraven made public the confidential complaint he had made to Latham Fish. He was now convinced, he said, that on the night before the first race the tender *Hattie Palmer* had come alongside *Defender* and "surreptitiously loaded" ballast aboard the yacht. During the race, he claimed, he noticed that "*Defender* was visibly deeper in the water than when measured." He could see, for example, that "a pipe amidships, which was flush with the water when measured, was nowhere visible." On the night after the race, Dunraven added, the extra ballast had been removed so that when the boat was remeasured her water line was roughly the length it had been at the time of the original measurement.

Dunraven followed the *London Field* article with a speech at Cardiff, Wales, in which he claimed that the New York Yacht Club had in effect confirmed its fraud by refusing a request he had made to have an observer put aboard *Defender* right after the race.

A howl went up from the New York newspapers that could almost be heard across the Atlantic. Dunraven later wrote that the "amount of excitement could not have been exceeded if some one had deliberately hurled an insult at the American nation." So loud were the wounded outcries from the United States that a few wags in the London Stock Exchange cabled their contacts in Wall Street to request that, if war were declared, the excursion steamers be kept out of the way of the Royal Navy. The Wall Streeters shot back that they hoped Britain's warships were better than her yachts.

"All very funny," wrote the mercurial Dunraven, "but not funny to me." His reaction, however, was benign compared to that of *Defender*'s afterguard. Oliver Iselin immediately dubbed Dunraven "a liar and a blackguard." He then wrote a seething letter to the race committee, demanding an investigation—"not alone to vindicate *Defender* and the honor of her owners," he said, "but also to refute the imputation cast upon the good faith of the club and the country."

The New York Yacht Club appointed a blue-ribbon panel, including

Some 20 white-togged crewmen tail on to the main halyards to hoist Defender's 8,000-square-foot mainsail under the critical eye of Captain Hank Haff, at the wheel. Haff hand-picked the men for the 1895 match from the young salts of Deer Isle, Maine, giving Defender the first totally American crew in Cup history.

industrialist J. Pierpont Morgan, former American Minister to Britain Edward J. Phelps, and eminent naval historian Alfred Thayer Mahan. It convened on December 27, 1895, in the Model Room of the clubhouse, and its hearings took five days. Dunraven crossed the Atlantic to present his case, but so great was the animosity against him that he was met by a pilot boat before his steamer docked in New York Harbor and was taken secretly to guarded rooms near the yacht club.

Accompanied by bodyguards, he appeared briefly at the club, but then returned to England without waiting for the verdict. The other witnesses, however, testified that no new ballast had been added. The *Hattie Palmer* had lain alongside *Defender* the night before the race, they admitted, but that was because, in preparation for the measurement procedure, she had put aboard some of the yacht's allowable ballast in the form of large pigs of lead. The lead could not, however, be properly stowed in that form. The tender had stood by while her crew had removed the ingots from *Defender*'s hold, cut the heavy metal into smaller sections and put it back. Latham Fish testified that Dunraven had not, despite his claim at Cardiff, requested that an observer be put aboard *Defender*. Committee members also swore that they had not heard of such a request until Dunraven mentioned it after he had returned home. Still other witnesses testified that the pipe referred to in the *London*

Topmast sagging, Defender (right) struggles onward with a dislodged shroud after Valkyrie III (center) brushed her at the start of an 1895 Cup race. "We will sail this race if we haven't a stitch of canvas," said Defender's owner, C. Oliver Iselin, as he followed Valkyrie around the course. He was awarded the race when Valkyrie was disqualified for the foul.

Field article was buried when *Defender's* ballast was moved about to adjust her tilt for the race, not by the addition of more weight.

Perhaps the most telling argument was made by *Defender's* designer, Nat Herreshoff, who pointed out that added ballast would have hurt rather than helped the yacht's racing trim and would have made the boat slower. On January 28, 1896, the panel finally pronounced its findings, in the most diplomatic language it could muster: "The committee are unanimously of the opinion that the charge made by Lord Dunraven had its origin in mistake."

American yachtsmen snorted and sniffed. Even some British yachtsmen suggested that Dunraven should simply acknowledge a mistake and apologize. Dunraven sulked. When the New York Yacht Club received no response to the committee's findings, its members voted to revoke the earl's honorary membership. Word of this action evidently reached Dunraven prematurely, because he publicly announced his resignation before the New York Yacht Club's letter reached him. And the New York Yacht Club members resigned themselves to the demise of international—at least British—competition for the America's Cup.

In the New York Yacht Club's Model Room, Lord Dunraven (right) voices his complaints about the 1895 race at a hearing attended by his racing opponent, C. Oliver Iselin (standing with his back to the window), financier J. Pierpont Morgan (far right) and naval historian Alfred Thayer Mahan (next to Morgan).

Fitful progress toward the ideal racing yacht

AMERICA 1851

OVERALL LENGTH: 102 ft. 3 in.
WATER-LINE LENGTH: 89 ft.
BEAM: 22 ft. 6 in.
DRAFT: 11 ft.
DISPLACEMENT: 146 tons
SAIL AREA: 5,263 sq. ft.

"The evolution of yacht design," American naval historian Howard Chapelle wrote in 1935, "has not been a logical and steady series of improvements." Indeed, progress toward the ideal racing vessel as typified by America's Cup defenders has been fitful, with many a false start, because the forces influencing yacht design have worked in unpredictable combinations.

Each of the defenders depicted here—the dates indicate the years that they raced for the Cup—embodies innovations that resulted from a complex interplay of factors. Their forms reflect the peculiar genius—or purely subjective whims—of the designers, the effects of changes in rating regulations that control dimensions and, to an increasing degree in the later vessels, advances in technology.

One of the farthest-reaching breakthroughs came fully 19 years before the first defense of the America's Cup, with designer George Steers's brilliant idea of applying the clipper bow to the yacht America herself (above) in 1851. The schooner's long, slightly concave bow astonished yachtsmen accustomed to the bluff nose of the traditional yacht, and her ability to slice neatly and speedily through the water touched off the quest for the ultimate racing machine.

Refinements in hull form continued to preoccupy designers as they began to experiment with America's Cup entries. Hull configuration, in fact, became the source of a design controversy during the 1870s and 1880s. In one camp were ranged advocates of the traditional American sloop—the broad, shallow, centerboard vessel that had proved its efficiency in windward performance. Equally ardent support-

ers of the British racing cutter—labeled the "cutter cranks" by their opponents—claimed superior speed for this narrow, deep-keeled yacht. The argument raged until a new generation of designers began to use elements from both types. The result was a series of elegantly proportioned hybrid sloops typified by Puritan (right), Edward Burgess' swift and seaworthy America's Cup defender for 1885.

Simultaneously, American designers confronted dictates other than their own inventiveness. In 1887 the New York Yacht Club's new specifications limited the length of a Cup contender's water line to 90 feet. Since speed is directly proportional to the square root of the water-line length, this could have meant slower yachts—but designers soon began to exploit a loophole that would determine the form of America's Cup racers for the next 18 years.

The officially defined water line was measured when a boat was on an even keel. At the bow and stern, however, a hull sloped up and out above the water line, and when a yacht heeled in the wind some of this extra length was submerged. By extending the bow and stern overhangs, designers in effect gave their yachts longer water lines—and thus greater speed—without violating the rules.

At the same time, the designers took advantage of the fact that the rules did not specify displacement. The underbodies of racing yachts were cut away drastically, to reduce the total surface area in contact with the water and, as a result, diminish frictional resistance. In this fashion, the so-called skimming dish, a vessel that was shaped roughly like a shallow, elongated saucer, assumed precedence in United States yachting.

A parallel development was the tendency, clearly apparent in the 1899 defender Columbia, to design for progressively larger amounts of sail, producing some of the greatest spreads of canvas yet seen in the America's Cup races.

The combination of huge sail area and relatively flat, light-displacement hulls produced boats that proved as unstable as they were swift. (The most extreme example was Herreshoff's 1903 Cup defender, Reliance, pages 108-111.) A demand for more seaworthy contenders resulted in a new rating system—the universal rule, promulgated in 1905—that legislated the skimming dish out of existence.

This regulation established a pattern that has characterized the subsequent history of American yacht design. Fuller-bodied hulls have prevailed, as the focus of innovation has shifted toward systems of rigging. Technological developments—most notably the introduction of light but strong alloys such as duralumin, used in the mast of the 1930 defender Enterprise—and increased understanding of the aerodynamic principles determining sail efficiency have continued to advance the yacht designer's art.

***PURITAN* 1885**

OVERALL LENGTH: 94 ft.
WATER-LINE LENGTH: 81 ft. 1 in.
BEAM: 22 ft. 7 in.
DRAFT: 8 ft. 8 in.; with centerboard, 20 ft.
DISPLACEMENT: 140 tons
SAIL AREA: 7,982 sq. ft.

With a proportionately deeper hull than those of the traditional wide, shallow American yachts of her era, Puritan reflects the influence of narrow, deep-bodied British cutter design. But she retained the centerboard—a characteristic feature of sloops sailed in the shallow waters off America's Eastern Seaboard.

VIGILANT **1893**

OVERALL LENGTH: 124 ft.
WATER-LINE LENGTH: 86 ft. 2 in.
BEAM: 26 ft. 3 in.
DRAFT: 13 ft. 6 in.; with centerboard, 24 ft.
DISPLACEMENT: 96 tons
SAIL AREA: 11,272 sq. ft.

Vigilant's pared-down underbody and pronounced overhangs identify her as one of designer Nathanael Herreshoff's celebrated racing machines. Another innovation that contributed to her speed was an exceptionally smooth hull of Tobin bronze, a heat-rolled metal that was stronger than ordinary bronze.

***COLUMBIA* 1899, 1901**

OVERALL LENGTH: 131 ft.
WATER-LINE LENGTH: 89 ft. 8 in.
BEAM: 24 ft.
DRAFT: 19 ft. 3 in.
DISPLACEMENT: 102 tons
SAIL AREA: 13,135 sq. ft.

*Columbia had a deep keel weighted
with 90 tons of ballast to stabilize
her sharply undercut hull. To compensate
for the keel's heaviness, designer
Herreshoff pioneered many weight-saving
innovations in the components of
the hull structure, including "bulb angles"
—light but strong framing members.*

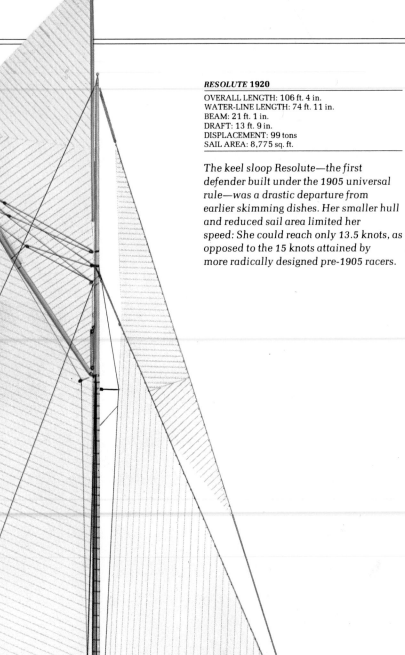

RESOLUTE 1920

OVERALL LENGTH: 106 ft. 4 in.
WATER-LINE LENGTH: 74 ft. 11 in.
BEAM: 21 ft. 1 in.
DRAFT: 13 ft. 9 in.
DISPLACEMENT: 99 tons
SAIL AREA: 8,775 sq. ft.

*The keel sloop Resolute—the first
defender built under the 1905 universal
rule—was a drastic departure from
earlier skimming dishes. Her smaller hull
and reduced sail area limited her
speed: She could reach only 13.5 knots, as
opposed to the 15 knots attained by
more radically designed pre-1905 racers.*

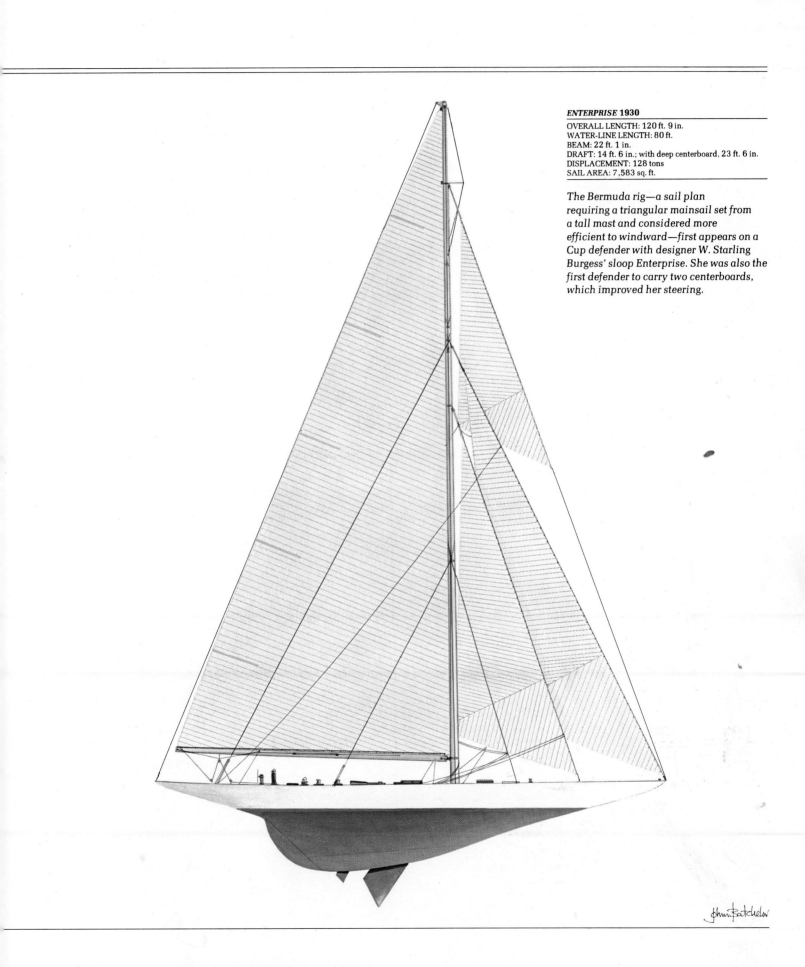

ENTERPRISE 1930

OVERALL LENGTH: 120 ft. 9 in.
WATER-LINE LENGTH: 80 ft.
BEAM: 22 ft. 1 in.
DRAFT: 14 ft. 6 in.; with deep centerboard, 23 ft. 6 in.
DISPLACEMENT: 128 tons
SAIL AREA: 7,583 sq. ft.

The Bermuda rig—a sail plan
requiring a triangular mainsail set from
a tall mast and considered more
efficient to windward—first appears on a
Cup defender with designer W. Starling
Burgess' sloop Enterprise. She was also the
first defender to carry two centerboards,
which improved her steering.

Chapter 4

A jovial tea merchant's pursuit of "the ould mug"

Amid welcoming vessels, Sir Thomas Lipton's green-hulled Shamrock reaches New York in 1899, opening a new, cordial era in America's Cup racing.

or three years the New York Yacht Club remained resigned to the possibility that there might never be another British challenger for the America's Cup. Then, on August 6, 1898, its members received an unexpected cable. The Royal Ulster Yacht Club in Belfast, Ireland, was inquiring if the Americans would entertain a challenge from one of its members, Sir Thomas Lipton. The cable ushered in one of the most glorious periods in the history of the Cup—and an era that was deliciously ironic. Between 1899 and 1930, the animosities between American and British yachtsmen were swept away and the true spirit of competition was restored to yacht racing by a grocer who knew virtually nothing about sailing—much less racing.

Thomas Lipton was the second son of an impoverished Irish family who had immigrated to Scotland during the potato famine of the 1840s. In 1860, at the age of 10, he left school to help support his family; at 15, he went to the United States, where he worked in tobacco fields and rice paddies, and as a peddler, a plantation bookkeeper and finally a New York City grocery clerk. In 1869 he triumphantly returned to Glasgow with $500 in his pockets. Two years later, at 21, he opened his first grocery store; at 30, he had a chain of more than 20 shops.

Every bit as much a freewheeling entrepreneur as the captains of industry he had admired in the United States, Lipton expanded his business from groceries into the international tea trade, buying up depressed plantations in Ceylon until he became the foremost tea merchant in the world. A teetotaler who never gambled on games of chance, he bet fortunes on new business ventures, inspired by the heady stimulation of competition. His enormously prosperous enterprises made him a multimillionaire by the time he was in his mid-40s. In 1897, when Alexandra, the Princess of Wales, started a charity to feed London's poor and ran short of funds, Lipton stepped in with a single check to make up the shortfall, earning the enduring gratitude of the Princess and bringing him to the attention of her husband, the future King Edward VII. Lipton received his knighthood shortly thereafter.

His philanthropic gesture catapulted him into a whole new world. His name, being the trademark of a national commodity, was famous throughout Britain. But Lipton himself, a bachelor who had lived wholeheartedly for his work for decades, was a fresh face to the Prince and his fun-loving circle. The lively tea merchant, with his direct, engaging manner and puckish sense of humor, was a virtually made-to-order companion for Edward, who had a liking for what his more austere mother, Queen Victoria, regarded as the more raffish section of society. The two men became fast friends, and Lipton—whose motto had always been There's no fun like work—found himself having a great deal of nonwork fun in an opulent playground of country estates, royal residences, racecourses and yacht clubs.

He discovered that he loved having a good time—and providing one for others. He gave lavish parties for his new friends at his home, Osidge Park, a grand estate outside London that acquired the nickname "Sausage Park" for the meat he sold in his grocery stores. And he bought a 1,240-ton steam yacht to which he gave the fine Irish name of Erin, then

Tea merchant Sir Thomas Lipton, who challenged for the Cup five times, sports a yachtsman's togs and an amused eye in this 1901 watercolor from the British magazine Vanity Fair. *The publication credited the self-made multimillionaire's business success to "Irish ambition, Scottish abilities and British pluck."*

took Europe's royalty out for cruises. But as a companion to the Prince, who was an ardent sportsman and an enthusiastic member of Europe's aristocratic yachting community, Lipton soon became swept up in the excitement of sail. Although he was no yachtsman—and never would be—he could afford to buy and race the best sailing yacht that Britain's shipwrights could produce, and he proved to be as ambitious a sportsman as he was a businessman. As his very first racing venture, he decided to try for yachting's most coveted prize—the America's Cup.

Happily, a Cup challenge could even combine sport and business. Lipton owed much of his success to a genius for advertising and promotion. "Laddie, it's like this," the Glasgow-reared Irishman once explained to a young yachting friend in his best music-hall accent. "When a chicken lays an egg, she cackles an' tells the whole farmyard. But when a duck lays an egg, she makes no' a sound. An' how many people eat ducks' eggs? Did ye never ask yourself yon question?"

With an eye always to developing new markets for his tea, Lipton calculated that the United States—not noted as a nation of tea drinkers—was ready. How better to promote his product than to take advantage of the publicity surrounding America's Cup matches and make the Lipton name a household word in the New World? "I think I'll have a shot at the ould mug," Lipton announced to friends in 1898. The Prince of Wales enthusiastically fell in with the scheme, promptly ordering the royal yacht *Britannia* to be fitted as a trial horse for the challenger his new friend ordered built.

Not all of Europe's aristocratic yachtsmen were as taken with Sir Thomas and his America's Cup ambitions as was the Prince. Kaiser Wilhelm of Germany, Edward's nephew, particularly disapproved of his uncle's friendship with Lipton. One day at Cowes the Kaiser was asked the whereabouts of the Prince. "They tell me he has gone boating with his grocer," the German monarch sniffed. On another occasion, when Edward nominated Lipton for membership in the Royal Yacht Squadron, the squadron's members discreetly suggested that it would be wise to withdraw the candidacy of a mere tea merchant rather than suffer the indignity of his being blackballed. Their royal affiliate tactfully withdrew Lipton's name.

The members of the New York Yacht Club, on the other hand, were not put off by Lipton's humble background or by his lack of yacht-racing experience. Although some grumbled privately about being used in a scheme to promote the sale of tea, most were overjoyed to have a bona fide challenge for the America's Cup, and their experiences with contentious yachtsmen must have made the jovial landlubber's bid even more attractive. Lipton, who looked back on his years in the United States with nostalgia and viewed Americans with affection, had been upset by the antagonism aroused by the Earl of Dunraven. As if to counter the earl's accusations of foul play in the 1895 match, Sir Thomas announced before leaving for New York in 1899: "There is no country in the world where a British subject will receive more true kindness or be more certain of getting better or fairer treatment than at the hands of our American cousins." This enduring affinity for the United States would sustain him through five challenges over 31 years and make what became known as the "Lipton Era" an exceptionally felicitous period in Anglo-American yachting competition.

Lipton's first challenger, designed by a celebrated third-generation Scottish boatbuilder named William Fife Jr., was called *Shamrock*. She was a long, lean beauty. Her water-line length was 89 feet, and she measured 128 feet overall. She had manganese-bronze bottom plating and a keel that extended just over 20 feet below her water line to balance the wind-filled weight of sails that reached almost 140 feet into the air. She was a pure racer rather than a practical yacht, and proved to be so delicate to handle—her steel mast had so much play that she wore out six separate suits of sails in her first year—that the New York Yacht Club agreed to modify its rules and permit her to be towed across the Atlantic rather than insist that she sail to New York.

Shamrock's American opponent, *Columbia*, was the third Cup defender designed by Nat Herreshoff and was an even more extreme example of the gradually evolving racing machine than *Shamrock* was (pages

Fashionable Mecca for yachtsmen and socialites

Cowes Week, said *Yachting World* in 1894, presented a "scene unparalleled in any other country—a million of money afloat and double the amount of happiness ashore."

Such was not always so. In the early 19th Century, Cowes, a diminutive seaport on the rustic Isle of Wight, had been what one visitor described as a "half-civilised resort of rough sailormen." That was before the Prince of Wales—later King Edward VII—frequented the Royal Yacht Squadron's annual August regatta there in the 1860s. Until the Prince became a regular, the regatta had attracted only a handful of yachting enthusiasts. But wherever the King went, high society followed and lesser mortals trailed.

At times the races were eclipsed in the public eye by the balls and lawn parties. During the day the Royal Yacht Squadron lawn bloomed with the "fairest and finest women of two hemispheres," said one writer; another claimed for that sward a dubious distinction as "a marine Madame Tussauds," because of all the celebrities there to be gaped at. By night yachts in

the Solent became a "flotilla of flame," as hundreds of lamps gave Cowes a charm that "Venice in the days of the Doges could not have presented."

Many Cowes aficionados deplored the changes that popularity and publicity brought. Cowes Week, said one disgruntled participant, seemed "no longer a small party who came down to live seafaringly, but a large crowd of new people who flit in and out of the little town with the one object of showing dresses, seeing the latest beauties, and keeping clear of the hated sea." Fashion extended even to the visitors' taste in dogs, as fox terriers, schipperkes and collies succeeded one another in favor from one summer to the next; in 1894, noted *Yachting World*, "poodles were clearly in the ascendant."

But if the fashionable scene diverted attention from the contests on the water, it did nothing to devalue the status of the exclusive circle of yachtsmen at the center of Cowes Week activities: the Royal Yacht Squadron. Well into the 1920s it was said to be harder to win membership in that club than in the House of Lords.

90-95). She was made of bronze, was more than three feet longer than *Shamrock* and had a deeper, narrower keel. Inside her hull, reported one observer, were only "steel beams, braces and emptiness."

Shamrock reached New York Harbor in mid-August 1899, towed most of the way by *Erin*. The sociable Sir Thomas could hardly have arrived at a better time. The Spanish-American War had just ended and New York was celebrating the American victory with characteristic enthusiasm. Lipton scarcely set foot aboard *Shamrock*, instead spending most of the next two months attending parades, dinners and concerts, and ferrying New Yorkers out to *Erin*, where he entertained them with an ever-open bar and all the tea they could drink. For a while the match seemed almost a secondary event.

A five-race series had been planned for early October, but *Shamrock* and *Columbia* waited through nearly two weeks of calm and fog before the first race was finally run on October 16. Then they sailed in light breezes, although they still had to work their way through heavy fog. A

Cowes Week visitors crowd the waterfront to view the yachts, in this turn-of-the-century photograph. At right, steamers deposit still more spectators.

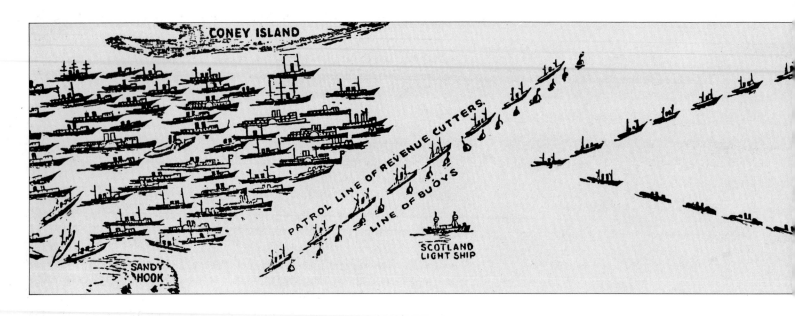

stronger wind finally rose and the fog lifted during the final leg; *Columbia* showed that she could sail better upwind than *Shamrock*, and won by 10 minutes 8 seconds.

During the following day's race, the yachts were buffeted by heavy gusts, one of which snapped *Shamrock's* topmast and carried away her topsail. Captain Archie Hogarth put her into the wind to see if she could be jury-rigged, but the damage was beyond immediate repair and the challenger retired, giving *Columbia* a second win. Lipton's yacht finally showed her stuff in the third race, soaring along at 13 knots in a strong northerly. But *Columbia* was even faster, winning by 6 minutes 34 seconds in a roaring finish.

Lipton could have given a reasonable alibi for losing his first challenge: Designer Fife, who had been counted on to assist in the afterguard, became ill and missed all of the races. But the jovial challenger made no excuses. At a farewell banquet, surrounded by his new admirers, he announced: "Gentlemen, I shall be back." New Yorkers were already calling him "the world's best sportsman."

He was back in 1901, as soon as the rules allowed. His second challenger was designed by George Watson, who had designed the royal yacht *Britannia* and Lord Dunraven's three *Valkyries*. Watson devoted a full 12 months to experimenting with paraffin models of hulls in a testing tank before coming up with the design for *Shamrock II*. The result, wrote the marine editor of *Scientific American,* was "the most refined form ever seen in a Cup challenger." At 137 feet overall, with an 89-foot 3-inch water line, the second *Shamrock* was longer than her predecessor and had a nearly flat body with a keel so deep and narrow that it resembled a fin.

A month after *Shamrock II* was launched in the spring of 1901, Sir Thomas proudly took his royal crony, Edward VII—who had been crowned King that January—aboard his scientifically designed new yacht for a trial race at Cowes. *Shamrock II* evidently needed more development. As she was maneuvering into position for the start of the race, a

Treasury Department cutters and Navy torpedo boats protect Columbia and Shamrock from excursion craft in this sketch of crowd-control plans for the 1899 Cup races. Congress authorized the government patrol in 1896, a year after spectator boats had interfered with the Defender-Valkyrie III match.

The New York Journal illustrates Columbia's statistics in terms of beer barrels, horses and pretty girls. The newspaper called the 1899 defender "the largest and costliest vessel ever designed for sport" and noted that her lead keel "outweighs the ammunition that sank the entire Spanish fleet at Santiago."

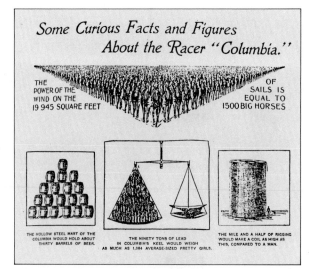

SANDY HOOK LIGHT SHIP.

F.A.Stevens

sudden gust twisted her steel mast and bent it double. Spreaders and spars cascaded onto the deck, narrowly missing the King. After ducking into the companionway, His Royal Highness helped the crew haul in the debris, then calmly lit a cigar.

Because of this embarrassing accident, Lipton was granted a one-week delay in the starting date for the Cup races. *Shamrock II* was rerigged, fitted with a wooden mast, and was ready to leave for New York at the end of July. Then, on the eve of departure, some of her crew decided to strike for higher pay. Lipton fired them and hired new men, and *Erin* towed the challenger across the Atlantic, arriving in mid-August 1901. On September 6, as *Shamrock II* was still tuning up for the first race, President William McKinley was shot; eight days later he died. Such events as yacht races had to be postponed while the nation mourned. *Shamrock II* did not have her chance until late September.

Her opponent was the same *Columbia* that had defeated the first *Shamrock*. Nat Herreshoff had designed a new racer, *Constitution*, but *Columbia* had consistently beaten her in trial races and had been selected to defend the Cup for a second time. Lipton, who by now had a highly developed case of Cup fever, was delighted at the news. He felt sure that his newer, more radical yacht had a good chance of beating old *Columbia*. And by now, many Americans were rooting for the smiling challenger. The editor of the American yachting magazine *The Rudder* put his sentiments about the race ahead of chauvinism and wrote: "For the sake of the sport I would like to see Sir Thomas Lipton win. As it is, the contest is too one-sided, but if the Cup could be passed and repassed across the ocean it would be better for yachting on both sides."

As the series started, it seemed as if that would happen. *Shamrock II* took the lead in the first race, proving that she could sail closer to the wind than *Columbia* could. This all-important advantage had Lipton partisans cheering as *Shamrock* led to the turning mark. But then *Columbia*, spreading everything she had, came racing down the homeward leg before the wind, slowly overtook the challenger and finished ahead of her. Evidently *Shamrock II* had paid for her gain in weatherliness—her ability to sail close to the wind—with less speed downwind.

Three days later, *Shamrock* led *Columbia* again, only to have the wind die and the race called off. When it was resailed on October 3, *Columbia* once more demonstrated her superior overall speed. With a strong wind batting the big boats over onto their sides, she thundered through the foam to victory.

Shamrock was still not through. Behind *Columbia* at the start of the third and deciding race, she caught up with and passed the American, rounding the mark 49 seconds in the lead. *Columbia* soon pulled abreast of the Briton, and challenger and defender came thrashing down the homeward leg almost bowsprit to bowsprit, spray cascading up their masts. They crossed the finish line with *Shamrock* two seconds in the lead. But because of her slightly smaller sail area, *Columbia* had been given a 43-second time allowance, and she was declared the winner by 41 seconds.

Sir Thomas was blithely optimistic, and had reason to be. All three races had been extremely close. In 90 miles of racing, his *Shamrock II*

Shamrock II lies in the mud, anchored by her fallen mast (left), after a sudden gust brought down her rig during a trial run off Cowes in 1901.

had lost by a total of only three and a half minutes. "The shamrock has three leaves," Sir Thomas reminded his cheering American friends. "Next time, for sure."

By the time he was back for his third challenge, in 1903, he was being hailed all over the United States as "Sir Tea," and Americans were referring to the trophy as the Lipton Cup. Lipton was in his glory—judging beauty contests, dining at the White House with President Theodore Roosevelt and visiting Boston, where he praised the intelligence of pre-Revolutionary War Bostonians who had dumped three shiploads of tea into the harbor, because "it wasn't Lipton's." He entertained almost constantly aboard *Erin*, giving lavish dinners and, of course, teas—at which champagne was also served.

The American press, always well represented at his parties, responded with glowing columns. A sharp-eyed journalist and social reporter named Dorothy Dix, writing in the effusive style that was her trademark, gushed in the New York *Journal* over *Erin's* drawing room filled with statuary, the music room with a harp and canaries, the dining room that could seat 70, the bedrooms "all done up in dainty lace and silk like a beauty's boudoir," and concluded that her host was "a three-volume romance bound in yachting flannels."

Not the least of Lipton's appeal to Americans was the fact that he was a bachelor, and although he stoutly maintained that he was not in the market for a wife, there were flurries of speculation about his matrimonial prospects. Anyone who read newspapers or magazines or watched newsreels could immediately identify the sprightly man with the crisp goatee, the rakish yachting cap, the polka-dotted tie and the gold watch chain across his dark flannel vest.

Lipton's third challenger, *Shamrock III*, was designed by William Fife Jr. with George Watson's help. She was, one yachting expert wrote, "quite the most beautiful that ever raced for the Cup." She was similar in shape to the first two *Shamrocks*, following the evolutionary trend of the time toward light and lively vessels with large amounts of sail. She was not, however, as radical in design as some of the American racing yachts of her era.

The New York Yacht Club's rating rules, under which Cup contenders raced, taxed water-line length and sail area but did not impose restrictions on the shape of the hull or take displacement into account. Designers were thus free to take enormous liberties with the hulls, cutting away the underbodies, lengthening the overhangs at bow and stern, and producing freaks so specialized that few were useful for anything but sailing for the Cup. They were mammoth examples of what became known as skimming-dish yachts—extremely light, highly tuned, undependable and dangerous in all but the most skilled hands.

Nat Herreshoff was commissioned by a syndicate of 10 wealthy New York businessmen and given carte blanche to design the 1903 Cup defender. The Wizard of Bristol, taking advantage of every design loophole in the prevailing rules, produced *Reliance (pages 108-111)*, the ultimate skimming dish, a craft so extreme that one yacht designer called her "perhaps the most wonderful and useless racing machine known to yachting." The lines that made her so fast also made her visually unap-

Old Britty: a beloved royal winner

Every now and then a ship is born that dazzles her public like a superstar. Such a vessel was *Britannia*—a yacht that had a 43-year career, the abiding affection of two Kings and the adoration of the whole British public.

One reason for her popularity was that she excelled as a racer; she sailed in 635 races and took a record 231 first prizes. Such was her charm that when she did lose nobody held it against her: At 42 years of age she lost at Cowes *(below)*, but King George V ordered the crew paid as if she had won.

This cynosure of racing yachts was built in 1893 at the command of the Prince of Wales—later King Edward VII—who wanted a yacht on which he could have a hot lunch while racing. He got that—and much more. *Britannia*, 121½ feet overall, was a floating palace equipped with such luxuries as a bathroom and a saloon with a piano.

The Prince delighted in his new vessel, but after five years it seemed she had served her purpose. From Cowes to Cannes, she had taken almost every sailing trophy worth having and had won £10,172 in prize money. Moreover, smaller racers were gaining favor. So in 1898 the Prince sold her. He soon changed his mind and bought her back as a test horse for Sir Thomas Lipton's *Shamrock*, then preparing for the America's Cup challenge in 1899.

Later, the Prince used her for his frequent visits to the Mediterranean. After 1901, when he acceded to the throne and became admiral of the Royal Yacht Squadron, he always watched the Cowes races from *Britannia*. His son George V, known as the sailor King, loved the big yacht as much as Edward had and periodically im-

proved her racing rig (she underwent six changes during his reign).

Before he died in 1936, George V ordered that *Old Britty*, as she had come to be called, should be spared the indignity of the wrecker's yard and instead be given a sea burial. And so, at midnight on July 9, 1936, with her old crew members on hand to witness the rites, she was towed by two destroyers from the Solent into the English Channel. The destroyers then withdrew as a preset charge exploded and sent *Old Britty* to the bottom—wearing on her prow a funeral wreath of flowers that symbolized the sorrow of the adoring public she left behind.

In this painting by an admiring artist, Britannia leads in a race at Cowes in 1935, her last year as a competitor. The 42-year-old vessel, outclassed by newer boats, actually won no races that year.

pealing; she was widely considered the most awkward-looking racer of her era. At 144 feet overall, she was the biggest Cup defender built up to that time and carried a greater area of sail than had ever before been piled onto a single mast: 16,160 square feet, 2,000 more than *Shamrock III* carried. Her huge size meant that she was handicapped with a time penalty of 1 minute 57 seconds. But that made little difference. In the 1903 series she ran away from *Shamrock III* in three successive races, leaving the challenger utterly lost in the fog in the last contest.

Having done her job in defending the Cup, *Reliance* retired permanently from racing and two months later was broken up for scrap. But her demise was small consolation to Sir Thomas, who considered *Shamrock III*'s humiliating defeat by the inelegant *Reliance* "the greatest disappointment of my life." Although he was not a gambling man, he declared that he would have been "willing to bet the *Erin*" that his beautiful yacht would take the 1903 series. "Give me a homely boat," he wailed good-naturedly, "the homeliest boat that ever was designed, if she is like *Reliance*."

Lipton was still eager to try for the Cup, but 11 years would pass before he would cross the Atlantic with another challenger. After the 1903 contest, the New York Yacht Club as a whole adopted a new rating system, called the universal rule, that took displacement and hull shape into account and effectively outlawed highly specialized, unseaworthy skimming dishes such as *Reliance*. The new system was soon in general use for yacht races throughout the United States and a similar rule was adopted in Europe.

However, the club's America's Cup committee took exception, feeling bound both legally and by tradition to its old deed of gift specifications. It argued successfully that the America's Cup was unique and therefore should be exempt from the universal rule. But Sir Thomas balked; he did not intend to pay for yet another delicate yacht tailored to the committee's demands and usable nowhere but in America's Cup racing. He issued challenges in 1907 and 1912 for matches—under the new rule. Both were refused. By 1913, however, he was so restless for the excitement of another shot at the "ould mug," that he gave in: He offered an unconditional challenge. The mercurial committee thereupon responded by giving him exactly the terms he had been asking for all along. The universal rule would obtain.

Jubilantly the perennial challenger commissioned his fourth Cup yacht—and got the "homely boat" he had joked about after his defeat in the 1903 series. *Shamrock IV*, blunt-nosed and bulky, looked so peculiar that even her designer, Charles E. Nicholson, called her the "ugly duckling." Yachting experts agreed, writing that she resembled a "hammerhead shark" and was "without a doubt the homeliest yacht ever put in competition for the Cup."

It was to be a long while, however, before the ugly duckling was put into competition. She was en route to New York in the late summer of 1914 when World War I broke out in Europe. *Erin* towed her to Bermuda to escape attack by German warships, then sneaked her up to Brooklyn, where she waited out the conflict. (Meanwhile *Erin* steamed back to Britain, joined the war effort as a hospital ship, then served as a

The ultimate skimming dish

Racing-yacht designers always have made a living by tacking around the measurement rules, but no other man ever did it so deftly as Nathanael Herreshoff did in 1903 with *Reliance*, the biggest, fastest sloop ever to race for the America's Cup. While earlier skimming dishes—so called for their wide, shallow hulls—had used loopholes in the Cup rules, *Reliance* took the trend to its logical conclusion. "She is an overgrown, ugly brute," wrote Thomas F. Day, editor of *The Rudder*, "but beyond that she is a splendid conception, splendidly carried out. One cannot but admire Herreshoff's courage in daring to take the step he has."

Reliance was a masterpiece of technical finagling. When measured at her mooring, her water-line length was 89 feet 8 inches, just under the 90-foot maximum. But just above the water line she splayed out into huge overhangs, 28 feet long at the bow and 26 feet aft, giving her an overall length of 144 feet. When she heeled, the overhangs submerged and her true water-line length—a key determinant of speed—increased to 130 feet. To lessen displacement and drag, Herreshoff molded a scow-like hull, 25 feet 8 inches at the beam, with a shallow draft and flat undersides. Stability came solely from the fin keel, 100 tons of cast lead that extended 19 feet below the water line.

Her sails were just as extreme, stretching 200 feet from bowsprit to boom end. The pull of this expanse of canvas, 16,160 square feet all told, was so great that the largest halyards and sheets were made of four-inch manila rope. The mainsail was made of specially woven triple-O duck about one eighth inch thick.

With her radical hull and clouds of canvas, *Reliance* heeled to her sailing lines in a mere seven-knot breeze, would bury her lee rail in a 12-knot blow, and could make 15 knots on a reach. But she also manifested the faults inherent in a rule that favored such fair-weather craft. Even as she trounced *Shamrock III*, *Reliance* was acknowledged to be an unseaworthy freak. "It is time to call a halt when 135-foot yachts cannot go out in a breeze of over 12 knots strength without danger of losing the entire rig overboard," wrote one yachting authority.

Two months after defending the Cup, *Reliance* was broken up for scrap. And for the next Cup race, the New York Yacht Club adopted a new rating formula, the universal rule, intended to produce "a wholesome type of yacht" by penalizing overhanging ends, light displacement and excessive sail area. The designer who devised the new rule was the same one who, with *Reliance*, had made hash of the old one: the Wizard of Bristol, Nathanael Herreshoff.

The key to Reliance's soaring rig
was her telescoping topmast, a patented
Herreshoff invention. In strong winds
the wood topmast was kept down inside
the tubular-steel mainmast, but in light
airs a belowdecks winch ran the topmast
up. The club topsail shown here, its
jack yards attached to the topmast and
gaff, extended Reliance's rig still
farther, towering 175 feet above the water.

RELIANCE

Reliance's speed did not result from her radical shape alone. Beneath the highly polished skin of ³/₁₆-inch bronze plates, the yacht was a tour de force of structural and mechanical engineering.

To lessen his boat's displacement and thus reduce the amount of water she had to shoulder aside, designer Herreshoff saved on weight until her framework looked more like that of a modern airplane than a turn-of-the-century sailboat. The hull's key structural members were T-shaped web frames 8 inches wide, made of ⅛-inch nickel steel and spaced 80 inches apart; at 20-inch intervals between them were flimsier L-shaped frames of 2-inch steel.

To support the tremendous weight of the mast, Herreshoff built an enormous steel keelson beneath it and added extra web frames on each side *(inset, below)*. The yacht's fragile skeleton was stiffened by a latticework of steel reinforcements, including transverse braces of steel tubing within the web frames. The deck, made of ¼-inch aluminum plates, was laid over a network of ⁵/₁₆-inch steel straps, then covered with a ⅛-inch layer of cork linoleum to provide a good foothold.

In his quest for lightweight construction Herreshoff overlooked nothing. Rather than use stock hardware, he specially designed every cleat, hook, shackle and turnbuckle, par-

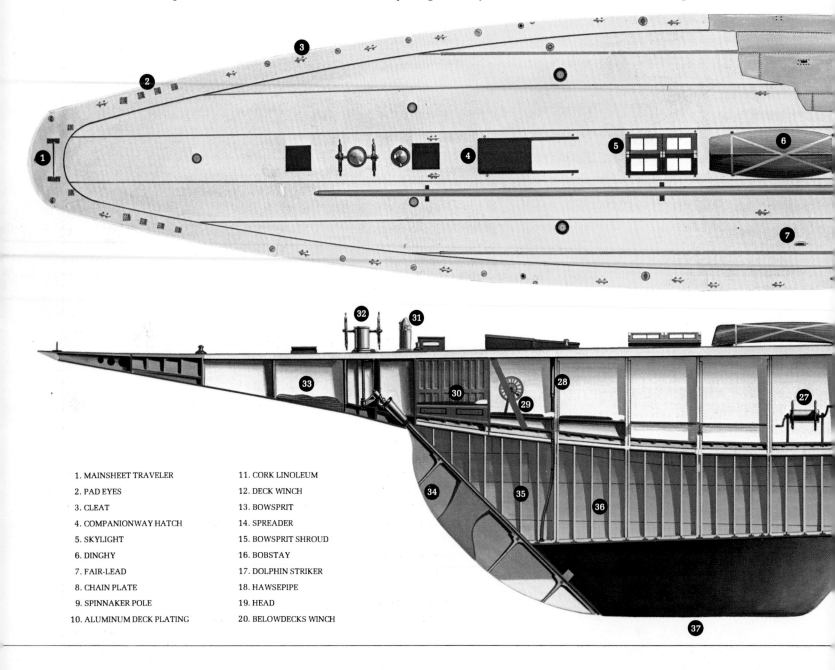

1. MAINSHEET TRAVELER
2. PAD EYES
3. CLEAT
4. COMPANIONWAY HATCH
5. SKYLIGHT
6. DINGHY
7. FAIR-LEAD
8. CHAIN PLATE
9. SPINNAKER POLE
10. ALUMINUM DECK PLATING

11. CORK LINOLEUM
12. DECK WINCH
13. BOWSPRIT
14. SPREADER
15. BOWSPRIT SHROUD
16. BOBSTAY
17. DOLPHIN STRIKER
18. HAWSEPIPE
19. HEAD
20. BELOWDECKS WINCH

ing away pounds or ounces anywhere he could. To ensure that the spars and fittings retained sufficient strength, he tested prototypes to their destruction on three machines in his home and shop.

The hallmark of Herreshoff's genius was the machinery he designed for *Reliance*. He introduced a foot-operated brake on the steering gear to lighten the helmsman's task in an hours-long race and an on-deck indicator that showed the exact angle of the rudder. The hollow rudder itself contained a true Rube Goldberg contraption: a rubber bladder that could be filled with air by a foot pump when *Reliance* carried a lee helm, so that—at least in theory—the added

buoyancy aided the struggling helmsman; with a weather helm, the bladder was emptied and the rudder filled with sea water. And where other racing yachts trimmed their sails primarily with raw on-deck muscle, Herreshoff led halyards and sheets belowdecks through fair-leads to nine two-speed, self-releasing winches, each designed for its particular task.

With this quantum jump in yachting technology, the crew of *Reliance* handled her sails so neatly that other boats looked slow and sloppy by comparison. And the winches were so well designed that identical machines were used on America's Cup defenders for the next 34 years.

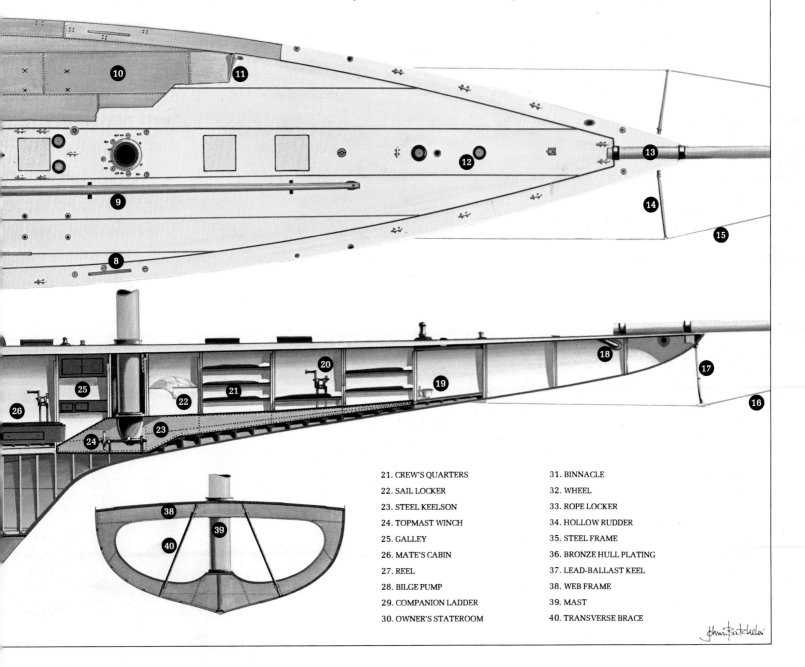

21. CREW'S QUARTERS	31. BINNACLE
22. SAIL LOCKER	32. WHEEL
23. STEEL KEELSON	33. ROPE LOCKER
24. TOPMAST WINCH	34. HOLLOW RUDDER
25. GALLEY	35. STEEL FRAME
26. MATE'S CABIN	36. BRONZE HULL PLATING
27. REEL	37. LEAD-BALLAST KEEL
28. BILGE PUMP	38. WEB FRAME
29. COMPANION LADDER	39. MAST
30. OWNER'S STATEROOM	40. TRANSVERSE BRACE

John Batchelor

patrol boat in the Mediterranean, and finally was sunk by a torpedo.)

Not until 1920 did *Shamrock IV* have her chance against defender *Resolute (page 94)*, which was designed by Nat Herreshoff and skippered by a future U.S. Navy Secretary, Charles Francis Adams. For a while it appeared that Sir Thomas' hope of winning the big trophy would be fulfilled at last. *Resolute* broke her mainsail gaff's attachment to the mast and had to withdraw from the first race, giving it to the challenger by default. *Shamrock IV* won the second race commandingly. Posing for photographers, Sir Thomas practiced "lifting the cup," in this case a cup of Lipton's tea. His ugly yacht clearly was capable of taking the series. In the third race she again took the lead and was a quarter of a mile ahead, when *Resolute* slowly began to close on her. The defender passed *Shamrock*, then *Shamrock* caught up and passed *Resolute*, crossing the line ahead of her, but by only 19 seconds. Because she was much larger than her opponent, *Shamrock IV* had been burdened with a huge time handicap of seven minutes one second. *Resolute* was declared the winner of the third race. In a thrashing, windy fourth race, with the yachts thundering alongside each other at 12 knots, *Shamrock* lost again and the series was at a tie.

It seemed as if all business ceased in New York on July 24. For the first time in Cup history a five-race series had reached the fifth race, and crowds of spectators turned out to watch the deciding contest and cheer *Shamrock IV* on. But that day the winds piped up to near gale force, and when the committee boat signaled the captains to suggest calling the race off, both agreed.

Sir Thomas, watching from a chair aboard his new steam yacht, *Victoria*, came closer than he had in 21 years of racing to losing his temper in public. He ordered *Victoria's* launch to take him out to *Shamrock*. The yacht's captain, William Burton, explained that he had been genuinely afraid he would lose the boat in the open Atlantic in such a wind; the cabin was flooding and one of his afterguard had reported from below that the yacht was about to break up. Lipton, clearly aware that his captain was the one to make such a decision, but still angry, went back to *Victoria*. He permitted himself only a muttered comment that "Shamrock had much worse weather than this coming over," and then kept his silence. Two days later, in shifting, tantalizing breezes, *Resolute* drifted to victory 13 minutes 5 seconds ahead.

For the first time, Lipton betrayed an air of defeat. He did not join the American critics who berated the "paper-napkin sailboats" that could not race in a 30-knot wind, nor the British yachting writer whose indignation led him to blame the Americans for being afraid their "cockleshell was unable to stand up against a summer squall in a sheltered bay." But there were no more genial promises of coming right back with another *Shamrock*. Lipton waited nine years before making a formal move toward another challenge. Meanwhile, there were some important new developments in yacht design that would lead to some equally important changes in the nature of America's Cup competition.

Designers had responded to the widespread acceptance of the universal rule by constructing racing craft in which length, sail area and hull shape were balanced to produce safer, more seaworthy boats. Most clubs were now also requiring racing yachts to conform to complicated sets of measurements—called rules of scantlings—that determined the size and strength of a vessel's structural components, further ensuring its seaworthiness.

The new rules—which would soon apply to all races, including the America's Cup—went hand in hand with a new rating system that established standardized classes of racers, designated by water-line length. While there was room for variation, the limitations imposed were such that any yacht built to a specific rating under the universal rule would be so similar in design to any other yacht in its class that no more handicapping would be needed.

Ever since about 1830, when the Royal Yacht Squadron had tried equalizing the chances of all the vessels in club races with handicap allowances, yachtsmen had been fighting over rules. Making an accurate measurement of each yacht's capabilities on the basis of size and sail area was extremely complicated—especially since designers competed to find ways of getting around the rules. Handicapping especially puzzled landlubbers who watched yacht races without knowing which contestant had actually won, since the first boat across the finish line might "give time" to a dozen others. And handicapping particularly frustrated Sir Thomas Lipton. Had it not been for the handicap, *Shamrock IV* would have taken the Cup home in 1920, and *Shamrock II* might have won it in 1901. One reason for his delay in challenging for a fifth time was his hope that some sort of class system could be established for America's Cup races, and that the yachts could simply race boat against boat, with no time allowances given to either.

During the same period, sails and rigging had undergone a dramatic evolution. Since the turn of the century, yachtsmen on both sides of the Atlantic had been experimenting with a new rig that would eventually replace the traditional gaff-rigged topsail and mainsail—which had a heavy upper spar, clumsy mast rings and bulky mast attachment—with a single triangular sail that rose straight to the top of the mast. The British called this new arrangement a Bermuda rig because a similar one had been used on that island for two centuries. In America it was soon called the Marconi rig, after the Italian inventor of wireless telegraphy, because the many shrouds needed to stay the new mast made it resemble a transmitting tower. A large jib overlapping the mainsail was later added to the new rig; since it was first used in a regatta off Genoa in 1927, it became known as a genoa and eventually got the nickname jenny.

The new rig found its finest application in the huge racing yachts built under the universal rule for what was alphabetically designated the J class—boats with a 75- to 87-foot water line. Nothing like the J-boats had ever been seen before; no yachts so awesome have been built since. Only 10 of these soaring beauties were ever constructed; and by 1940, changing world economic conditions would make them obsolete. But while they lasted, they were the glorious epitome of the racing yacht.

In 1928 the America's Cup committee announced that boats for the next match could be built up to the J-class rating under the universal rule, would be required to conform to rules of scantlings, and would race

The prolific wizardry of Captain Nat Herreshoff

In the late 19th Century, Captain Herreshoff points out the yacht-building operations in his company's Bristol, Rhode Island, shipyard to two unidentified companions.

Of all the sea-loving men who have put their minds and hands to the art of boatbuilding, few have made such an impact as Nathanael G. Herreshoff—a lanky, laconic designer who revolutionized the American racing yacht from his Bristol, Rhode Island, workroom. Known to friends and family as "Captain Nat" and to racing enthusiasts of more than a quarter-century as the "Wizard of Bristol," Herreshoff designed and built the five yachts that successfully defended the America's Cup against six challengers (one of his boats raced twice) between 1893 and 1920. His vessels not only excelled, but set the standards for future yachts, and many of the features he originated remained in use long after his time.

For a man who was so crucial to a sport that was nothing if not sociable, Nat Herreshoff himself was singularly reclusive. In 1894, when the 1893 Cup winner Vigilant went to England for a series of races, Herreshoff went along to supervise her fitting out. One day the Prince of Wales came aboard and asked to see the designer, but Herreshoff, not wanting to have to make small talk even with a royal visitor, fled to the engine room and stayed out of sight until the future King Edward VII departed.

Herreshoff spoke so tersely to newsmen who were seeking stories that they found him forbidding. And he was nearly teetotal: Even his friends and family knew him to take a drink only once—when his Columbia beat Sir Thomas Lipton's Shamrock in 1899.

Herreshoff was a long time getting down to the work that made him famous. In 1878, at the age of 30, he joined the Bristol shipbuilding firm founded by his brother John, and for the next several years concentrated on designing steam launches and boilers, many of them for the United States, British, French, Russian and Peruvian navies. From time to time the Herreshoffs turned out a pleasure vessel, and one they built in 1891, the sloop Gloriana, won so many races that the Herreshoffs came to public notice.

The following year a group of powerful New York financiers asked them to undertake a yacht to defend the America's Cup in 1893. Nat swiftly designed and built Vigilant (page 92), and after she won the name of Herreshoff was irrevocably linked with sail. In less than a decade the two brothers were building pleasure craft for racing enthusiasts all along the Atlantic Coast.

Nat's work habits were as eccentric as his social behavior. He worked at home (in a house he designed himself), usually putting in seven 12-hour days a week. Every morning or evening he made an inspection tour of the boatyard. When he indulged himself in relaxation it was for a busman's holiday: He took his family sailing on Narragansett Bay.

His design for each yacht began with a pencil sketch on an 8-by-10½-inch pad, in which he worked out the overall length of the finished yacht, the length at the water line, and the draft, beam and freeboard at three points. From this sketch he built a wooden model. His specifications then went to the Herreshoff yard. It often required three or four draftsmen to keep up with him; after he died, at the age of 90, he left a file of some 18,000 of his sketches. Not every sketch or model was turned into a finished yacht, but enough were built to keep 200 pattern-makers, foundrymen, blacksmiths, machinists and carpenters employed full time producing his boats.

At Captain Nat's instigation, the boatbuilders did the initial work of hull construction with the keel up—a novel procedure that required considerably less scaffolding than the old method, with the keel down, and therefore saved time, materials and space in the workshop. The Herreshoffs followed other farsighted and time-saving practices as well. They kept a large inventory of all kinds of wood—oak, pine, teak, butternut, cedar, cypress, white pine, mahogany, spruce and Douglas fir. When the need for a particular wood arose, there was no wait for an order to be filled. Similarly, the yard had its own foundry and turned out custom-made bronze hardware that included bronze bow chocks, which spared the wooden hull from the erosive effects of lines slipping in and out.

The Herreshoff yard built yachts faster and in greater numbers than its competitors. A customer could order a boat in the winter and expect to sail it in the spring. But it was more Herreshoff's imaginative advances in design than speedy delivery that drew customers to the yard.

Among his innovations was the ballast keel, which was made of lead and significantly lowered the center of gravity of a boat, enabling it to safely carry more sail in strong winds than could a vessel with an unballasted keel. He also developed crosscut sails—sails cut on the bias of the fabric—which could bear tremendous wind stress without stretching out of shape; hollow spars that reduced the weight abovedecks; hollow, lightweight bronze rudders, with interior chambers that could be flooded with sea water when more heft was needed for heavy going; and, to facili-

tate fixing the sails in position, track slides like the one later carried on *Enterprise* (page 118).

In 1920 Captain Nat saw *Resolute*, his last America's Cup defender, win at New York. By now his brother John was dead, and Nat himself was in his seventies. He thereupon retired and sold most of his interest in the company. But the yard continued operating, with his son Sidney serving as chief designer and Captain Nat himself serving as consultant until he died in 1938. After World War II, businesses that depended on such individually hand-crafted products as Herreshoffs' could no longer survive economically, and the company shut down. When the last yacht—bearing work order No. 1521 and symbolically named *Memory*— was launched in 1946, she marked the end of 83 years of Herreshoff expertise. Although Captain Nat was long dead, the vessel bore many earmarks of his design style, still carried the Herreshoff name—and had the distinctive bronze fittings that marked it as a product of Herreshoff wizardry.

America's Cup defender Reliance comes down the Herreshoff ways into Narragansett Bay in 1903, as eager spectators watch.

without a time allowance. The new conditions had scarcely been announced when a Lipton order went to designer Charles Nicholson's
Portsmouth harbor boatyard: Build *Shamrock V* as a J-boat.

The Americans, at the height of their giddy 1920s prosperity, responded with overkill. Not one but four new J-boats, at a cost of more than half
a million dollars each, were commissioned by four syndicates of wealthy
New York and Boston businessmen. As the huge racing vessels were
being built, the stock market suffered its calamitous 1929 crash. But few
wealthy American yachtsmen foresaw the magnitude of the coming Depression; most were confident that what was happening on Wall Street
was a temporary aberration in the economy and they saw no reason to cut
back on their expenditures.

Construction of the expensive mammoths went ahead according to
schedule, and the summer of 1930 saw one of the most spectacular
yacht-racing displays of all time: four great, gorgeous J-boats competing
for selection to defend the Cup. As a result of these trials, it was Lipton's
ill fortune to find himself confronted with two of the most remarkable
men in the history of American yachting: W. Starling Burgess and Harold S. "Mike" Vanderbilt.

Boston-born Starling Burgess, the son of Edward Burgess, designer of
the Cup defenders of 1885, 1886 and 1887, was every bit as brilliant as
his father and a much more sophisticated naval architect. A pioneer in
the new field of aviation, he had piloted the first aircraft in New England,
had won a number of flying trophies and had built warplanes for England during World War I. He was among the first yacht designers to
recognize how the principles of aerodynamics that dictated the shape of
a plane's wing also applied to a yacht's sails. He also wrote and published poetry, and was particularly proud of his ability to recite an entire
Swinburne ballad while perched on his head (he maintained that the
rush of blood to his brain stimulated his memory cells).

Burgess was commissioned by one of the New York syndicates, and
immediately did something rare for a yacht designer of the time. He
constructed two large models, each nine feet long with a 15-foot mast,
and secretly tested them in the waters off Provincetown, Massachusetts.
The results of these tests were incorporated in a 15-foot-long scale model, which he tested in a towing tank. Burgess then made studies of his
sails in a wind tunnel, and conducted hull and mast tests in an engineering laboratory at the Bureau of Standards. When he was finally ready to
build his full-sized Cup defender, Burgess turned to the Rhode Island
yard of the Wizard of Bristol. Although Nat Herreshoff himself had retired at the age of 76, after nearly 40 years of building racing yachts,
he was on hand to advise Burgess during the construction of the young
designer's defender.

She was named *Enterprise*. In the exciting three-month series of selection trials in the summer of 1930, she clearly demonstrated her superiority over the other three contending J-boats and was chosen as the Cup
defender. *Enterprise* was a wonder to behold. When Lipton arrived in
the United States in August 1930 and saw his *Shamrock V's* opponent
for the first time, he was appalled. Although the new rules might have
produced a seaworthy boat, they had not outlawed the racing machine.

Enterprise was the ultimate modern example. Eighty feet long at her water line, she had a 162-foot mast and a heavy keel with two center-boards to make her easier to steer: a deep, 14½-foot one for sailing into the wind and a shorter, four-and-a-half-foot one for reaching and running before the wind.

But what particularly amazed Lipton and other traditional yachtsmen were the innovations in Enterprise's rigging. Her great mast, tapering from one and a half feet in diameter at the base to nine inches at the truck, was made of two hollow tubes of duralumin, and at 4,000 pounds weighed less than two thirds as much as Shamrock V's hollow wood mast. The Enterprise's "tin mast," as it was called, was secured by more than 80,000 rivets and had so many supporting stays and shrouds doing such a delicate balancing act that Burgess added a device called a shunt dynamometer—an instrument normally used to measure and adjust cable tension in bridge construction—to give the crew accurate measurements of the strain on each stay at any given time.

Burgess had provided two dozen winches to handle Enterprise's lines. Most were belowdecks, where eight crewmen—who became known as the black gang, after the coal-begrimed stokers on steamships—worked

A diagram from a 1930 issue of the Illustrated London News shows some novel features of Shamrock V, that year's America's Cup challenger. One valuable innovation was a belowdecks winch (middle row, left of center) for hoisting and lowering the mainsail; it reduced the number of men needed for that job from as many as 30 to only two, and also kept the deck clear of rope.

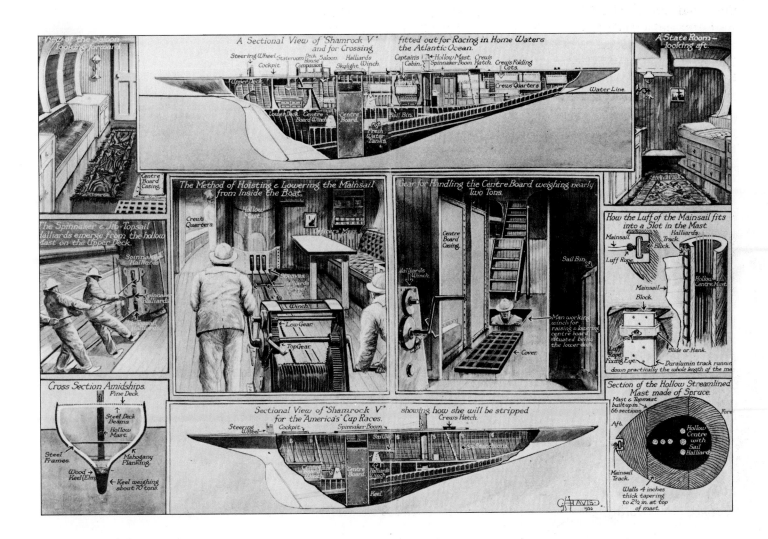

them on commands shouted from topside. But *Enterprise's* most astonishing feature of all was her radical "Park Avenue" boom *(right)*, which incorporated an arrangement of runners and slides that allowed fine adjustments to the curve of the mainsail's foot. In order to accommodate this system, the flat top of the boom was built so wide that two men could stand on it abreast—hence its name.

The dramatically innovative racing yacht was perfectly designed for the skipper her syndicate had chosen. In fact, he had proposed many of the innovations. Harold S. Vanderbilt, great-grandson of shipping and rail magnate Commodore Cornelius Vanderbilt, was an amateur, but only in the strictest sense of the word. He was a man with enormous energy who applied a superb analytical mind to his twin preoccupations: bridge (he invented contract bridge) and yachting.

Vanderbilt set a new pattern for America's Cup skippers, and not only because he was one of the first amateurs in a position that thereafter would be dominated by amateurs. He brought a thoroughly systematic attitude to the job. He had spent his entire yachting career in big boats, to which he introduced the methods of the corporation board room, assembling an efficient afterguard in which each member was assigned a specific responsibility and either discharged it to the chairman's satisfaction or was put ashore. Under Vanderbilt's command, everything functioned so smoothly and each crewman did his job so well that the skipper was completely free to concentrate on steering the boat. Vanderbilt had nearly perfected the technique of the full-speed start, calculating the timing of his pregun maneuvers with such precision that in most of his races he was able to hit the starting line at high speed almost at the moment the gun went off.

Standing stiffly behind the wheel, flawlessly attired in white flannels, blue blazer and club tie, his hand on the delicately balanced helm, Vanderbilt sailed almost by feel. He had learned through long experience how to adjust the helm and sails to get the maximum speed out of any combination of wind and seas. Clustered around him was a subcommittee of his afterguard; they constantly monitored the force and direction of the wind, the boat's position and movement, the set of her sails, and her rival's relative position.

The 1930 series, which would be determined by four wins out of seven races, was to be sailed off Newport, Rhode Island. The waters off New York Harbor had become too encumbered with flotsam and, during races, too crowded with spectator craft to allow a safe, fair match. Also, the J-boats were so tall that they could not sail under some of the bridges in the East River. Vanderbilt ordered a thorough study of the wind patterns off Newport, including a U.S. Weather Bureau analysis of records for June through September for the previous 20 years. The report he received showed an average daytime wind velocity of a little over 12 mph during the summer months and slightly more in September. Vanderbilt accordingly was able to plan his tactics in detail well in advance of the race.

For all his coldly calculated strategy, Vanderbilt was acutely aware of how unpopular his mission was. He realized, he wrote a year after the match, that "the greater portion of American people would have

Two seamen inspect the end of Enterprise's 66½-foot Park Avenue boom. The foot of the mainsail was attached to slides that moved along the transverse runners. Once the sail had been bent into the desired aerodynamic curve, pegs were inserted in holes in the runners to keep the slides in position.

been glad" to see the Cup finally carried away by their beloved Sir Thomas Lipton. He and his fellow syndicate members, he added, "appreciated and in some respects shared the feelings of our fellow citizens." But Harold S. Vanderbilt had a puritanical sense of responsibility, and he was determined not to be the man who lost the America's Cup after three quarters of a century of uninterrupted American possession—no matter how much affection he retained for the happy Irish warrior opposing him.

As it happened, he did not have to worry. *Enterprise* won a clean sweep of four races against *Shamrock V*—one by default when one of *Shamrock's* halyards parted, forcing her to withdraw, the others by margins of 2 minutes 52 seconds, 9 minutes 34 seconds, and 5 minutes 44 seconds. As the victorious defender approached the finish line at the end of the fourth race, Vanderbilt graciously asked Burgess, who had created their spectacular yacht, to take her across. The designer took the wheel. "And *Shamrock V*, where is she?" Vanderbilt wrote later. "We look astern. She is about a mile behind, a badly beaten boat. Our hour of triumph, our hour of victory, is all but at hand but it is so tempered with sadness that it is almost hollow. Uppermost in our minds is a feeling of sympathy for that grand old sportsman." ⚓

Workmen at Ratsey and Lapthorn's sail loft in New York pull up the edges of Enterprise's 5,000-square-foot mainsail, which weighed about a ton. It was sewed of 18-inch-wide strips of Egyptian cotton that would have stretched a mile if extended lengthwise; one strip lies on the floor in the foreground.

An intricate meshing of gear and teamwork

The huge J-boats of the 1930s sacrificed simplicity to the demands of speed. To handle the large sails, the crew needed a great variety of special gear. While it was possible to trim small staysails on a simple winch, genoa and quadrilateral jibs were so big they had to be sheeted home by means of multigeared pedestal winches—nicknamed coffee grinders because of their large cranks that could be turned by four men at once.

No winch was strong enough to trim the huge mainsail against the force of the wind. Instead, as many as 10 men hooked its sheet to a web of lines and blocks called a grab tackle, which multiplied their brute strength up to 30 times. Spinnakers were gigantic and needed endless adjustments to keep them full (Ranger, the famed J-boat on which these drawings were based, had an 18,000-square-foot parachute spinnaker that was the largest sail ever made).

Aside from the special gear needed for the heavy work, a J-boat also carried many pieces of equipment that increased the precision with which the vessel could be sailed. The main boom, for instance, was fitted with an elaborate series of winches, blocks and wires so it could actually be bent nearly a foot to impart an aerodynamic curve to the foot of the sail. To ensure that the start of a race could be timed accurately, the afterguard—the skipper and his assistants who directed the paid crew—carried as many as six stop watches, all of which were meticulously synchronized. To guard against equipment failure, all crucial instruments such as compasses and speedometers were duplicated.

Maintaining all this gear and using it efficiently made the work of the afterguard and crew immensely complicated. Every one of the 30 or so men in the complement was rigorously schooled in the precise moves he had to make when the skipper ordered a jibe, tack, sail change or any of the other myriad maneuvers that had to be accomplished quickly and without flaw during a race.

Errors did occur, of course—and they were never ignored. "Emphasis was laid on mistakes, with a view to avoiding them in the future," said one J-boat owner, and successful skippers lost no opportunity to improve the expertise of their men. Advised one: "Drill, practice and drill, and practice again. Sail for as long as possible every day until you long for an excuse for a lay day."

Success depended on impeccable teamwork; each man had to mesh his efforts with those of his shipmates so that the whole operation proceeded with split-second timing, whether a job called for three crewmen to trim a staysail or for the entire team to man the winches and sheets to bring the boat about. And the fact that these drawings of a crew at work in an America's Cup race reflect orderly concentration rather than furious strain or individual heroics is a testament to just how practiced a great racing team could be.

Partly hidden by the boom, crewmen haul on a grab tackle to flatten the mainsail at the start of a race. During the 10 minutes before the starting gun, the crew might have to trim or slacken sails several times as the yacht jockeyed for position.

Coming to the line, the helmsman listens as the navigator, standing in a hatch behind his binnacle, reads time checks from a stop watch. The tactician, using binoculars at the starboard rail, adds a running update on the maneuvers of the opponent.

On the afterdeck, a winch gang tightens a jib sheet while the kneeling man nearest the helmsman turns a worm-gear winch to move the main sheet-block. Seated at the rail, an observer from the competition watches for infractions of the racing rules.

At the stern, crewmen stand ready at their tacking stations as
the helmsman prepares to bring the boat about. On the skipper's
command, the man kneeling at left will let go the leeward
sheet of the staysail; then the three men at far right will use bars to
turn the small winch sheeting the sail home on the opposite
side. Meanwhile, four more men (standing, left rear) will use two
similar winches to tighten the running backstays to give
the mast support from what will then be the windward side.

As the boat tacks, four hands at the bow pull the foot of the huge quadrilateral jib so the sail's wildly flapping clew, or lower aft corner, can clear the front of the mast as the sail passes over to the opposite side. Just behind the mast an afterguardsman turns a wheel to bend the boom away from the wind, thus giving the mainsail a more efficient shape.

With the boat now on the new tack, four crewmen sheet home the quadrilateral jib by cranking a coffee grinder. The coffee grinder, using a chain drive belowdecks, turns the winch drum around which the fifth crewman, called a tailer, has wrapped the tail of the sheet.

Getting ready for a run downwind, a
man (foreground, with his back to the bow)
attaches a spinnaker boom to the mast.
Behind him, another crewman begins to
tug the spinnaker up through the
forehatch as the sail is hoisted, and at the
bow two men attach a corner of the sail
to the outboard end of the boom.

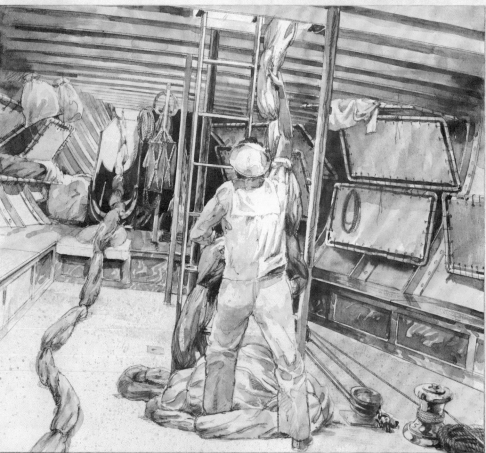

As the spinnaker is run aloft, a
crewman belowdecks guides the sail up
through the forehatch. Another
headsail (left), the canvas most likely to be
needed next in case of a wind shift, has
been threaded up into a sail chute at the
bow. The chute leads to the deck by
way of a hatch at the base of the headstay.

RICHARD SCHLECHT

Her spinnaker filled by the following wind, a mighty J-boat runs for the line. On her port rail, a man watches the sail closely, ready to signal aft for any necessary adjustments to its sheets. In the background, the opponent is just rounding the mark and raising her spinnaker, still held tightly bunched by lines called stops. When the spinnaker's sheets are pulled taut, the stops —made of easily broken string known as rotten-twine—will snap, and the loosened canvas will belly out with the wind.

ir Thomas Lipton's defeat in the 1930 Cup match seemed a melancholy and anticlimactic finish to a great era in yachting, one that like the period it spanned—and like Sir Thomas himself—had been characterized by seemingly boundless opportunity, optimism and extravagance. Lipton tried to remain cheerful, but the loss had been a crushing blow and now there was a bitter edge to his humor. After one of the races, he said to his afterguard, "Gentlemen, I have to congratulate you for having kept the *Enterprise* in sight the whole day through." He was 80 years old and beginning to show it. One of his American friends noticed that, for the first time, Sir Thomas did not recognize him. To the sympathizers who tried to console him, Lipton finally admitted, "I can't win. I can't win."

His gloom was suddenly dispersed by the actor and comedian Will Rogers, who (evidently at the suggestion of Lipton's public relations man) wrote a letter that *The New York Times* printed on its front page: "What do you say to this? Let everyone send a dollar apiece for a fund to buy a loving cup for Sir Thomas Lipton bigger than the one he would have got if he had won, contributed to by everybody that really admires a fine sportsman. Send it to Mayor Walker in New York. Let Jimmy buy it

Aboard Endeavour shortly before the first 1934 America's Cup race, owner-skipper T.O.M. Sopwith (behind life buoy) and his wife (in beret) are shown surrounded by the yacht's crew—most of them amateurs who were recruited less than two months before the series began. Sopwith had fired his professional crewmen when they went on strike for an increase in their £5-a-week wages.

Endeavour is pulled along by her parachute spinnaker, a relatively new kind of sail she used in the 1934 Cup races. The ballooning shape of the 12,000-square-foot spinnaker caught so much wind that it could run away with a yacht. Harold S. Vanderbilt, the American skipper whose Rainbow beat Endeavour that year, also used a parachute spinnaker and said that it was "rather terrifying to handle in a breeze."

and present it on behalf of everybody with an inscription along this line: 'To possibly the world's worst yacht builder but absolutely the world's most cheerful loser.' You have been a benefit to mankind, Sir Thomas, you have made losing worth while.''

In a little more than a week, 16,000 dollar bills poured in, and jewelers at New York's Tiffany & Company went to work making up a cup of 18-karat gold. A group of miners in Utah sent a silver base for it. The trophy was completed that November, and Lipton returned to New York to accept it. At the presentation he was so overcome with emotion that, probably for the first time in his garrulous life, he was unable to make his speech. What he did manage to say was this: "Although I have lost, you make me feel that I have won. But I will try again. Yes, I will try again."

He never tried again. He was corresponding with the New York Yacht Club about the possibility when, on October 2, 1931, at the age of 81, he died—only a few months after he had been honored by being elected at last to the Royal Yacht Squadron.

Harold S. Vanderbilt would defend the Cup again three years later—with none of the compunction he had felt when he had frustrated the dreams of the beloved boating grocer. He had every reason to expect the 1934 challenger to be the most formidable of them all. He was right.

Thomas Octave Murdoch Sopwith—generally known by his initials, T.O.M.—was an aeronautical engineer who had designed planes for World War I, the most famous being the Sopwith Camel. As a sportsman, Sopwith concentrated on yacht racing, applying his aeronautical knowledge and his considerable talent to become Britain's best amateur helmsman. Sopwith had raced both sailboats and motorboats in the United States and could be said to know American waters intimately, having been dunked unceremoniously into the Atlantic when one of his planes stalled off Coney Island in 1912. He had watched Lipton's final attempt, and as soon as the 1930 series was over, intending to contend for the Cup himself, he bought *Shamrock V* to gain experience in racing a J-boat. He wanted to make his challenge in 1932, but waited an extra year, at royal request.

Edward VII, who had encouraged both Lord Dunraven and Sir Thomas Lipton, had died in 1910. His son, George V, was an even more ardent yachtsman, but he sensed that in 1932 a diplomatic delay in challenging might be appreciated. The Depression had become a grimly realized fact in the United States, and as the King put it, "with industrial conditions as they are" in England as well, the enormous expenditures required for a Cup challenge might seem ostentatious. So in his capacity as admiral-commodore of the Royal Yacht Squadron, King George suggested that "this was not an opportune time" to make a challenge. It took Sopwith a year to persuade the King to relent. In 1933 the Royal Yacht Squadron, in Sopwith's name, forwarded its formal challenge: four out of seven races to be held in September of 1934.

Sopwith's challenger was *Endeavour*, a new J-boat created by *Shamrock V*'s designer, Charles Nicholson. She was 83 feet long at the water line and her body was built entirely of steel except for a wood deck, studded with four-speed winches. She also sported a sail called a quadri-

A French "grande dame" who outsailed the men

For close to three centuries no one would have disputed the claim that yacht racing was a gentleman's pastime. But in the 1920s there hove up on the horizon a female who not only competed in the sport, but excelled in it. She was Virginie Hériot, whom admiring Frenchmen nicknamed the "*grande dame* of yachting."

The daughter of a wealthy Parisian department-store owner and philanthropist, little Virginie first went on board the family's steam yacht as a small child—and fell so deeply in love with the sea that she virtually wedded herself to it for life. "The word 'passion' is inadequate to describe the feeling with which the sea inspired her," a friend recalled, "and she wanted to breathe it into everybody."

At first Virginie Hériot sailed only as an enthusiastic passenger. But in 1920, at the age of 30, she acquired a steam yacht of her own. Two years later, having decided to take up sailing, she bought the schooner *Meteor IV* from the recently deposed Kaiser Wilhelm II of Germany, and renamed the vessel *Ailée* (winged).

Over the next 10 years she had 11 more yachts built for herself. Showing a single-mindedness that characterized everything she did, she christened them all *Ailée* or *Petite Aile*, and distinguished one from another only by their numbers.

Handling the helm herself—at the time, still widely considered a strictly masculine skill—Virginie competed against men in international sailing regattas in France, Italy, Spain and England, winning trophy after trophy. And in 1928 she defeated the best male sailors in the world to take an Olympic gold medal in Amsterdam.

Virginie Hériot spent 10 months out of 12 afloat; when racing was out of season, she cruised. In one or another of her *Ailées* she made 17 cruises in

Yachtswoman Virginie Hériot stands amid nautical symbols in this 1930s watercolor.

the western Mediterranean, six in the eastern Mediterranean, nine in the Atlantic, 10 in the English Channel and the North Sea, and seven in Scandinavian waters, racking up a grand total of 143,232 miles.

She was also a dedicated, tireless proselytizer for the joys of yachting, giving 54 lectures and writing nearly a dozen books on the subject. "Instruction from the sea, that is my program," she averred. "To win ever more hearts to it, that is my goal."

In 1932 at Arcachon, on the Bay of Biscay, she entered the races celebrating the 50th anniversary of the local sailing society. She took the helm herself, but after a quarter of an hour of sailing she fainted. The following day, at the age of 42, she died; the cause of her death has never been explained, although it was probably a heart attack. The finale, however, was appropriate enough for this single-minded woman, who had vowed to go on sailing "right to the last breath."

lateral, a radical new four-sided jib that had been tested and perfected in a wind tunnel. Despite the growing worldwide depression, at least one other British yachtsman was able to race a J-boat that year. W. L. Stephenson's metal-hulled *Velsheda,* built by Nicholson in 1933 and dubbed the "steel-breasted beauty," sailed against *Endeavour* and gave her some tough competition before Sopwith left for America.

The Vanderbilt syndicate wanted to defend again, and promptly ordered a new J-boat. So great had been the outcry against *Enterprise's* many mechanical contrivances that members of the New York Yacht Club and some of their counterparts in Britain had met and agreed to outlaw the 1930 defender's double centerboard, her lightweight mast and most of her belowdecks winches. *Enterprise,* outmoded by the new rules, wound up being sold for scrap, and Starling Burgess went to work on a defender to be built in Nat Herreshoff's Bristol yard. He produced a yacht 82 feet long at the water line, with a duralumin mast heavier and sturdier than *Enterprise's* and a flexible, curving boom that required the constant attention of two crewmen. She was named *Rainbow.*

Rainbow seemed unbeatable in light airs. But in heavier weather she was beaten in the early trials by one of the 1930 J-boats, *Yankee.* It was a difficult decision for the members of the selection committee, even after *Rainbow* started winning a few windier races. But on balance they preferred *Rainbow,* and selected her over *Yankee.* Some New Yorkers predicted that this would prove to be a mistake.

The first race, on September 15, somewhat relieved the defenders' anxiety. In shifting light breezes, *Rainbow* took the lead from *Endeavour.* Then the breezes died to a near calm, and the race was called off. (But not before the captain of the U.S. destroyer *Manley,* pressing too close to the yachts in order to accommodate newsreel cameramen aboard, received a tart query from another spectator craft, financier Vincent Astor's steam yacht *Nourmahal:* "Are you challenging *Endeavour?*" The signal came from the destroyer captain's Commander in Chief, President Franklin D. Roosevelt, who was Astor's guest that day.)

The first race was finally completed on September 17. It was windy, *Endeavour* weather, and *Rainbow,* plagued by foul-ups and accidents to her spinnaker, lost by two minutes nine seconds. To the Americans' consternation, *Endeavour* won again the next day. In fact, she led all the way in a windy, three-hour-nine-minute race, the fastest one thus far in the history of Cup competition.

It looked as if this time the Cup really would go back to England. There was no doubt that *Endeavour* was the faster boat, whether beating to windward or running downwind. Her svelte four-sided jib (which her sailors called the "Greta Garbo") improved her upwind performance, though not a lot more than a similar jib—quickly made up by the Americans—improved *Rainbow's* performance. But *Endeavour's* huge, bulging spinnaker (which the sailors called the "Mae West") apparently could outdraw anything *Rainbow* had.

As for Sopwith, he was proving every bit as shrewd a helmsman as Vanderbilt, moving or tacking to cover (in effect, block) every attempt the American made to overtake him. The faster boat handled as well as, if not better than, the defender, but Sopwith's crew was not quite so skill-

ful as Vanderbilt's. Sopwith's professionals, like Lipton's in 1901, had gone on strike for more pay on the eve of departure from England. Sopwith had fired them and replaced them with amateurs. These were enthusiastic enough, but their spirit did not quite make up for their lack of experience; nor did *Endeavour's* afterguard run the boat with the ordered delegation of responsibilities that characterized a Vanderbilt yacht. The only specialist with clear authority was Mrs. Sopwith, who had been her husband's timer in countless other races.

After the first two races put *Endeavour* two up, New York bookmakers were giving 2-to-1 odds that the challenger would win. The third race took on an air of more excitement and suspense than any previous contest in America's Cup competition.

It was a two-leg race: 15 miles out to the stake before the wind and then back against the wind. Before the start, the two expert helmsmen maneuvered around each other like a pair of nervous dogs. Then Sopwith took off on the first leg well in the lead. *Rainbow's* crew could not get her troublesome spinnaker to set well, and *Endeavour* increased her lead. By

Rainbow, the 1934 Cup defender, beats through Atlantic waters. Her innovations included a boom that bent to give an aerodynamic curve to the mainsail.

In the crucial third race of the 1934 Cup series, British challenger Endeavour (blue) took the lead on the first leg (1) and was well ahead of Rainbow (red) at the mark (2). But on the homeward leg Endeavour turned to starboard to escape a calm spot (3), then tacked back so close to Rainbow that the air bouncing off the American's sails backwinded the challenger (4). Endeavour tacked twice more to get clear, but by then the defender had a commanding lead (5).

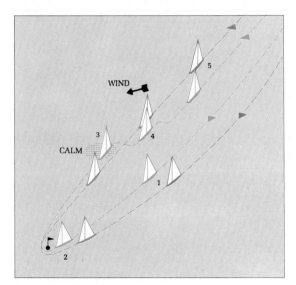

the time she reached the stake boat, 15 miles from the starting line, she led by a commanding 6 minutes 39 seconds.

Skipper Vanderbilt, erect behind *Rainbow's* big helm, was tight-lipped as his yacht rounded the turn and set out after *Endeavour*. In an upwind leg, with the light airs that prevailed that afternoon, *Rainbow* still had a chance, though a slim one with *Endeavour* so far ahead. But the wind had been slowly shifting from northeast to east-southeast and was now more off the beam—or to the side—than ahead. This meant the yachts were now on a close reach, which favored *Endeavour*, a fast boat on a reach. *Rainbow*, however, had one small advantage. The wind had shifted enough as she came around the mark that she was able to lay a course slightly upwind of *Endeavour's* course, and aimed more directly at the finish line (*diagram, left*).

For 10 minutes Vanderbilt nursed *Rainbow* along while his crew tried every possible trim of the sails to make the defender move faster. As he later wrote, "there did not seem to be anything I could do." *Endeavour* and T.O.M. Sopwith appeared to be an unbeatable combination. The America's Cup, he concluded, "was on its way back to England."

Standing beside Vanderbilt, diplomatically silent, was Sir Ralph Gore, the Royal Yacht Squadron representative assigned to sail aboard the defender. Vanderbilt handed the helm over to one of his afterguard, asking him to see if he "could make the darned thing go" (the height of Vanderbilt's profanity). He then clumped down the companionway, with Sir Ralph in tow, "to drown my sorrow in coffee and sandwiches."

The man to whom he handed the wheel was Sherman Hoyt, a short, bandy-legged naval architect and a veritable fox in the cockpit. Hoyt considered most British racing yachtsmen "luffing fools." If a competitor tried to go upwind of them, they immediately covered by luffing—going even closer upwind to block the competitor—even if doing so cost them valuable seconds. Hoyt had raced with and against Sopwith a number of times in England, and had noticed in Sopwith a strong penchant for covering.

Unfortunately for Hoyt, while *Rainbow* was on a slightly more windward course than *Endeavour*, the American yacht was so far behind that the Englishman had no reason to try to cover. But then a fluky wind favored Hoyt with an unexpected bonus.

A telltale patch of smooth water, indicating a soft spot, a small area of near calm, lay directly in *Endeavour's* path. Evidently Sopwith did not see it—or did not see it in time—because *Endeavour* sailed right into it. The challenger tacked to windward, both to seek stronger airs and to cover the now fast-approaching *Rainbow*. It proved to be a fatal mistake. Sopwith lost the momentum that presumably would have carried his big boat safely through the soft spot. Hoyt was gaining on him rapidly and with mounting hope.

Having crossed *Rainbow's* bow, Sopwith tacked again to set a new course for the finish line. But it was too late and he had lost too much momentum. *Rainbow* continued to gain, with every man in her crew—including the astonished Vanderbilt, who had rushed on deck to watch—perched on her leeward rail to give her the right balance. While Sopwith struggled to get *Endeavour* moving, *Rainbow*, with little Sherman Hoyt at the helm, glided past to leeward of the English yacht. *Endeavour* was backwinded, her sails caught in the wind deflected off the passing American yacht. Sopwith was forced to tack two more times to clear his sails of the turbulence, and he lost more precious minutes in the process. *Rainbow* continued serenely on course and came straight down to the finish line to win by 3 minutes 26 seconds.

The series now stood at two to one in favor of the challenger. But that race had altered the momentum of the series. Vanderbilt was barely ashore before he was on the phone to Frank Paine, a genius of the spinnaker who had helped *Yankee* nearly beat *Rainbow* in the trials. Would he bring his best spinnaker and join *Rainbow's* crew? Paine drove through the night to Newport, with *Yankee's* best spinnaker in the back of his car. Next day was a lay day to give the contending yachtsmen a chance to rest, but Vanderbilt and Paine used it to rerig *Rainbow* and increase her ballast. By the fourth race, the defender was ready with a much better behaved spinnaker.

The rest was anticlimax. *Rainbow* won the three final contests closely but conclusively. The fourth and sixth races were marred by near fouls and bitter protests over questions of right of way. Had it not been for the good sportsmanship of both Sopwith, who instructed his afterguard to be discreet, and Vanderbilt, who was lavish in his praise of Sopwith and *Endeavour*, America's Cup competition could have sunk nearly to the level of the Dunraven period. As it was, yachtsmen on both sides of the ocean agreed that the better boat had lost, because of the more skillful helmsmanship of the defenders. Designer Nicholson could not resist saying on his arrival home: "I have learned for the first time that the fastest yacht does not win the race." And Sopwith wasted no time in announcing that, like Sir Thomas, he would be back.

He came back in 1937, with another new J-boat, *Endeavour II*. The new *Endeavour* was a faster boat than her predecessor, and in trial races in England she proved that she was faster too than any of the existing American J-boats. But in America the economic depression was even deeper by that time, and the New York Yacht Club could not find enough wealthy yachtsmen to form a syndicate to build a new defender. So Vanderbilt undertook the defense out of his own pocket. His new J-boat, *Ranger (pages 134-141)*, was the work of Starling Burgess and a young designer named Olin Stephens, who subjected models of the proposed design to the most exhaustive tank testing that had ever yet been done for a J-boat. The result of their painstaking efforts was a steel-hulled vessel with a bulbous stem and a flattened stern—a shape that Burgess said was "so unusual that I do not think any one of us would have dared to pick her had we not had the tank results."

Ranger was built virtually at cost by a Maine shipyard whose employees were desperate for work. To cut down on his expenses even more, Vanderbilt had her rigged with secondhand fittings from his earlier defenders *Enterprise* and *Rainbow*. She turned out to be the greatest J-boat of them all, "totally different from any J-boat I had ever handled," wrote the delighted Vanderbilt. He dubbed his sleek, magnificent racer the "super 'J.'"

Ranger proved as super as her nickname in the 1937 match, utterly

A 1937 newspaper cartoon makes gentle sport of Harold S. Vanderbilt's Ranger for her hand-me-down components. In addition to using many secondhand items when fitting out the yacht, Vanderbilt had her rerigged with borrowed mast, shrouds and stays after she was dismasted shortly before the America's Cup selection trials.

outclassing *Endeavour II.* The challenger was beaten so badly in the first two races—by 17 minutes 5 seconds and 18 minutes 32 seconds respectively—that Sopwith had her hauled out of the water to see if a lobster pot had become entangled in her rudder; there was nothing. *Endeavour II* also lost the last two races, by 4 minutes 27 seconds and 3 minutes 37 seconds.

Ranger was not only the greatest but the last of her breed. Even at her bargain price she had cost around half a million dollars. And as the Depression wore on, no yachtsman, not even Harold Vanderbilt, could afford that kind of luxury. By the time the economy picked up, the graduated income tax, along with the higher wages demanded by the paid hands who were needed to handle the sails on the huge yachts, spelled the end of the glorious but prohibitively expensive J-boats. A handful of heirs to old fortunes and a few makers of new fortunes managed to continue racing large yachts. But by 1942, all of the magnificent American J-boats had finished their racing careers and had been broken up to make their contributions—in the form of scrap—to the Allied cause in World War II.

The end of the War brought more challenges and indications that, whoever won, the America's Cup races would probably go on forever. But the postwar challengers and defenders were much smaller, 12-meter yachts. With the end of the majestic J-boats, the grandest days of America's Cup racing were gone forever.

Vanderbilt stands at the helm of Ranger, flanked by the specialists of his crack afterguard: from left, Roderick Stephens, who as the "rover" took care of trouble-shooting assignments anywhere on the boat; assistant helmsman Olin Stephens; navigator Zenas Bliss; observer Gertrude Vanderbilt, who advised the helmsman of competitors' movements; and Arthur Knapp Jr., who trimmed the headsails and spinnaker.

134

The building of a crack racer

Designers Olin Stephens (left) and
Starling Burgess stand at their drawing
board in Bath, Maine, where they
supervised the construction of Ranger.

"We used to think of Ranger as the mechanical rabbit that always leads the greyhounds over the finish line," a yachtsman later reminisced about the J-boat that defended the America's Cup in 1937. "We had to think that or go out of our minds with frustration." Ranger was Harold S. "Mike" Vanderbilt's "ultimate conception" of a yacht, a boat so overwhelming that she won an incredible 32 of her 34 contests and never lost a one-on-one race.

She also won her opponents' awe-struck respect. To T.O.M. Sopwith, the owner and captain of Endeavour II, the 1937 challenger that she beat in four straight America's Cup races, Ranger's speed was simply "unbelievable," while Sopwith's designer, Charles Nicholson, called her lines the most revolutionary advance in hull design in half a century.

Ranger's spectacular success was largely the work of four men: Vanderbilt, her skipper and owner; Professor Kenneth

Davidson, the engineer who tested her; and, above all, W. Starling Burgess and Olin Stephens (left), her designers. Burgess had been designing airplanes and yachts (including the two previous Cup defenders) for some 30 years, but there was no doubt where his heart lay. "There's more money in planes," he said, "and more fun in yachting. I like fun, so that's that." The precocious Stephens had exploded onto the yacht-designing scene at the age of 23 in 1931, when an early effort, Dorade, won a transatlantic race.

For Ranger, Burgess and Stephens each designed two hulls, then joined Davidson to test five-foot wax models of the designs in a 100-foot towing tank to determine which was best at various speeds and angles of heel and yaw. The most radical design, model 77-C, won hands down.

"I do not think any one of us would have dared to pick her," Burgess admitted later, "had we not had the tank results and Kenneth Davidson's analysis to back her." The winning design was by Burgess—a fact that remained yachting's best-kept secret for 20 years because of an agreement between the two designers to share the credit. (Olin Stephens finally revealed in 1956 that Burgess was the principal designer, after a magazine article wrongly credited Stephens with the lion's share of the design.) Burgess gave Ranger a snub-nosed bow and rounded stem that increased deck space and saved weight. He also endowed her with a long, overhanging stern that extended her water-line length—and reduced leeway—when she heeled.

For the first time in 50 years, a Cup defender had no syndicate of backers, and even Mike Vanderbilt was short of ready cash during the Great Depression. A reduced bid persuaded him to build the yacht at Maine's Bath Iron Works, and the designers cut their fees to help him meet the cost of construction and the Cup campaign—some $500,000.

That sort of cooperation—and the cannibalization of past defenders (page 132)—sufficed to get Ranger constructed despite the hard times. And the extraordinary skill and harmony of Ranger's afterguard, whom Vanderbilt called his "happy family of six," assured her selection as the official Cup defender on July 6, 1937—Mike Vanderbilt's 53rd birthday. But they could not guarantee her a long life. Even harder times were to follow with the advent of World War II, and just four years after her single glorious season, Ranger was herself cannibalized as scrap for warships.

Ranger's lead keel hangs from a hoist
that will lower it into a construction cradle
at the Bath Iron Works. Weighing
some 110 tons, the keel gave Ranger the
high ratio of ballast to displacement
—about 70 per cent—that was a major
reason for her remarkable stability.

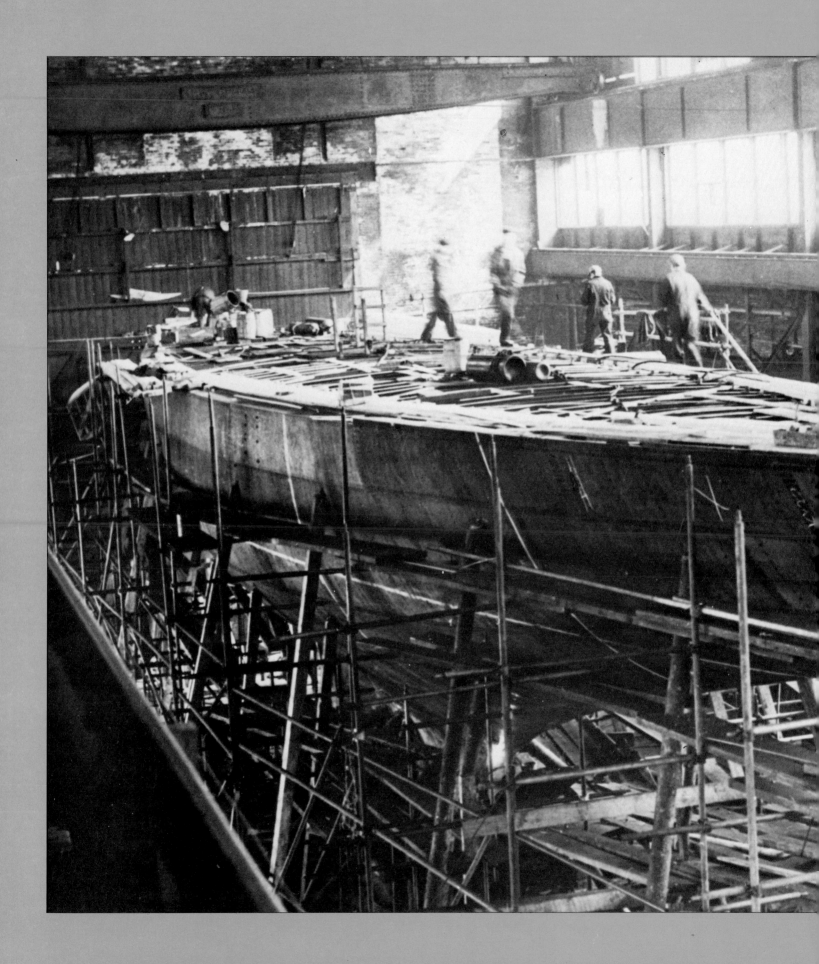

High above the shipyard floor, two
workers (right) balance nonchalantly on
the edge of Ranger's hull near her snub-
nosed bow. The plates of Ranger's all-steel
hull were flush-riveted rather than
welded, making her smoother and thus
enhancing her speed. Vanderbilt
heaped praise on Ranger's builders, who
"took infinite pains," he said, to
smooth the minutest dents in her plates.

138

Vanderbilt's wife, Gertrude—the
first woman to serve in a Cup defender's
afterguard—christens Ranger as
the yacht begins her slide (right) into the
Kennebec River on May 11, 1937.
The owner stepped Ranger's 165-foot
duralumin mast (seen lashed to her
deck at right) just after the launch so her
builders could see her in full glory. It
was an "expensive little thought," he later
wrote: The $15,000 mast broke off
while Ranger was being towed to Newport.

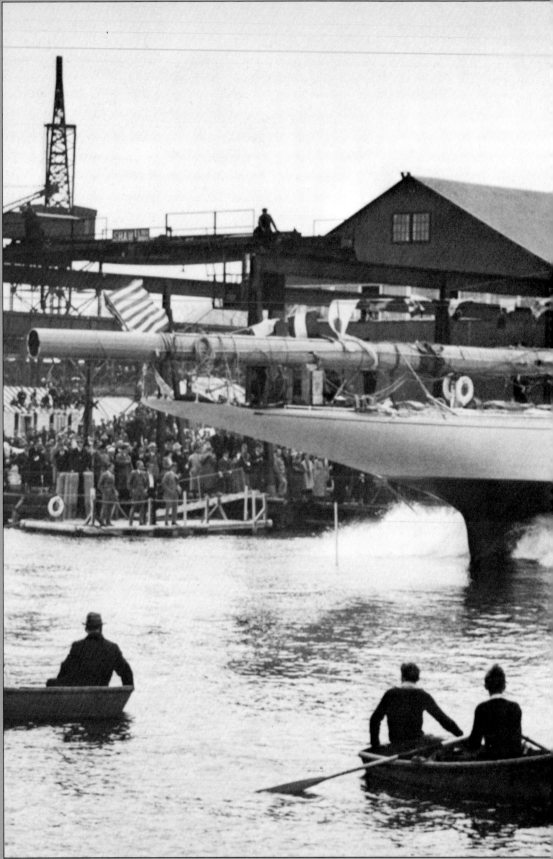

Twenty-one seconds after the gun—
and 18 seconds behind Ranger (left)—
challenger Endeavour II crosses the
starting line for the third race in the 1937
America's Cup match off Newport,
Rhode Island. Ranger extended her initial
lead, winning the race by 4 minutes
27 seconds, thanks in part to the greater
canvas she carried in her fore triangle.

A section of Ranger's hull sits in
Nathanael Herreshoff's Bristol, Rhode
Island, shipyard—where many
another defender was built—awaiting use
in 1941 as scrap for fighting ships.
Challenger Endeavour II fared better,
remaining afloat with a cut-down
rig as a cruising boat through the 1960s.

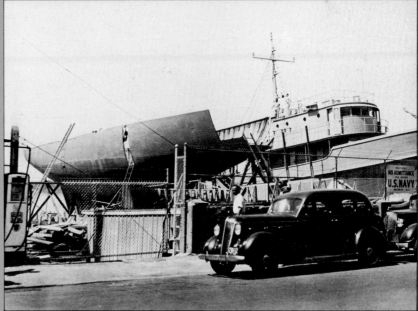

Chapter 5

High-seas tests of skill and courage

A t dawn on May 23, 1905, the three-masted yacht *Atlantic* was knifing through an easy sea under full topsails at 12 knots, far ahead of 10 racing competitors, when her crew sighted one of nature's most awesome creations. "There on our lee beam," recorded one of her company, "was a berg which must have been half a mile long and 300 feet high. It certainly was a beautiful sight with the morning sun reflecting from it." Beautiful, but dangerous: *Atlantic* steered well away from the shimmering floating mountain and sped on.

Before that sighting, icebergs were not, to say the least, a common hazard to racing yachtsmen. No contender had ever come within hundreds of miles of one during an America's Cup series or a Cowes Week regatta. But the 185-foot *Atlantic* was engaged in a new and different kind of contest. She was some 1,240 miles out of New York, her steel hull slashing through the North Atlantic's swells, in yachting's first officially organized ocean race. Just six days earlier, she and her companions, representing the United States, Britain and Germany, had crossed a starting line near Sandy Hook, New Jersey, and headed northeast on the great-circle route to the Lizard, a peninsula on the southwest coast of England, a distance of 3,014 miles. After more than two hundred years of sprinting around buoys, racing yachtsmen had finally set their compasses toward the blue horizon, where they would face greater tests of seamanship than rounding a mark—and greater dangers than being crowded by an overeager fleet of spectators.

Yachtsmen had pitted themselves against the open ocean before, of course. A few of the more adventurous were circumnavigating the globe in the 19th Century, and early challengers for the America's Cup had been required to sail across the Atlantic before they could take part in the races. But with the exception of a few privately arranged matches, which were usually sailed to settle personal bets, the pioneering bluewater yachtsmen were not racing, but cruising. Most of them prudently shortened sail every night, to minimize the risk of blundering into trouble in the darkness.

It was not until the the early 20th Century that a new generation of yachtsmen, eager to expand the boundaries of organized competition, turned the open sea into a racecourse. They took their inspiration from the old hard-driving captains of the clipper ships, who cracked on every stitch of sail their vessels were capable of carrying, during nighttime as well as daytime and in nearly all weather conditions. These sailors, most of whom were amateurs, also developed a revolutionary new breed of

Tethered to a stanchion by a safety line that hangs behind him like a tail, the helmsman of the American yacht Fleur de Lys *drives through a howling gale in the 1905 transatlantic race for the Kaiser's Cup. "We run like a scared dog— tremendous waves, splendid going!" noted Candace Stimson, daughter of the owner, as the schooner plunged eastward at speeds of up to 14 knots.*

high-performance ocean-racing craft, and with them they set record passages that astonished the old guard of millionaire yacht owners, professional captains and crews. But in their driving quest for thrills and glory, the offshore racers, as they came to be called, paid a price in lost vessels and drowned men.

The first formal ocean race, which brought the yacht *Atlantic* within sight of an iceberg, was an international event sponsored by Kaiser Wilhelm II as part of his effort to win recognition from the world's yachting community. The contest attracted 11 entrants from the United States, Britain and Germany. The vessels ranged in size from the 108-foot American sloop *Fleur de Lys* to the 245-foot square-rigged British yacht *Valhalla*. The only German entry, carrying the hopes of the Kaiser—though not carrying the Kaiser himself—was the 116-foot schooner *Hamburg*. A contestant to watch was the 150-foot schooner *Endymion*, whose young American owner, millionaire George Lauder Jr., had taken her across the Atlantic on a vacation jaunt five years earlier in the record-setting time of 12 days 19 hours.

But the favorite was the sleek *Atlantic*. She was two years old and in her prime. Her owner, American yachtsman Wilson Marshall, had invited six guests aboard for the transatlantic ride. Her professional crew was under the command of Charlie Barr, a famous skipper who had sailed three America's Cup defenders to victory, including *Reliance* in 1903.

The departure date, May 16, 1905, turned out to be so foggy that the start was postponed a day and the yachts went around into the lee of Sandy Hook at the entrance to New York Harbor. At 10 a.m. the next day, with the fog clearing before a light easterly, all 11 yachts were circling near the Sandy Hook Lightship. When the starting gun was fired at 12:15 p.m. New York time, the 127-foot yawl *Ailsa* led the pack, followed by the 135-foot schooner *Hildegarde*. *Atlantic* was the next to cross the line and set out for the coast of England.

On the first evening out, the contenders lost sight of one another in drifting fog. At sundown, however, the fog lifted and Barr, in *Atlantic*, caught a glimpse of the German schooner *Hamburg* as she eased past in the light wind. But the captain of the German yacht, Adolph Tietjens, opted for a more southerly course, and she gradually disappeared from *Atlantic's* sight.

For the next nine days, Barr pushed on to the east-northeast alone, flying everything that was in *Atlantic's* sail locker and constantly hounding the watch to trim and reset the yacht's canvas. During a single day the log keeper recorded these successive changes: "Set mainsail, maintopsail, both working staysails, jib topsail, and jib. Set balloon maintopsail. Took in raffee and squaresail. Set small spinnaker. Took in spinnaker, maintopsail, and jib topsail. Set No. 1 topsail and working maintopsail. Set squaresail and raffee. Took in squaresail, raffee, maintopmast staysail, topsails, and jib topsail. Squall struck at 8:30, so lowered spanker and mainsail. Squall passed so hoisted sails again. Bent squaresail and jibed."

Charging past the Grand Banks and averaging almost 220 miles per day, *Atlantic* kept to the great-circle route. For the six passengers, this part of the voyage was near-idyllic. On May 22, as the schooner passed

Across the Atlantic to settle a friendly little $90,000 bet

The first transatlantic yacht race resulted from a dinner party boast in October 1866, some four decades before any officially organized ocean racing existed. Over turtle soup at the august Union Club in New York, tobacco heir Pierre Lorillard declared to a group of friends that his new 105-foot schooner *Vesta* was the fastest yacht afloat.

Not so, retorted George and Franklin Osgood, owners of the 106-foot *Fleetwing*, and they put up $30,000 to prove it. Another yachtsman, James Gordon Bennett Jr., chimed in with a $30,000 bet on his 107-foot *Henrietta*.

News of the $90,000 contest set the sporting world agog. Never had such a sum been staked on any race. And what a race it would be: 3,000 miles from New York to the Isle of Wight. Moreover, the yachts would sail in winter, just as soon as they were ready.

On a bright, chill December 11, the three schooners assembled off Sandy Hook. The gun sounded and they were off, with *Vesta* in the lead. That night their courses diverged, and each yacht sailed on alone through gray, mountainous seas—"like new volcanoes after earthquakes," said a passenger—lashed by rising winds and snow.

Vesta and *Henrietta* took the northerly, great-circle route, steering widely separated but parallel courses and logging incredible runs of up to 280 miles a day. "This is yachting in earnest," noted *Henrietta's* captain, Samuel Samuels, who held the transatlantic packet record. Then, on December 19, a full gale ripped in from the southwest, and to keep from foundering, Samuels was forced to heave to. Even so, when he sighted England five days later, he trailed *Vesta* by only an hour. She too had been held up by the storm.

Fleetwing steered a more southerly route, seeking easier winds and a boost from the Gulf Stream. It was a shrewd gamble, but it did not work: The third day out a squall carried away her jib. Then, in the same gale that struck her opponents, an enormous wave broke over *Fleetwing's* deck, licked into her cockpit and flipped eight men over the side. Two clung to ropes and climbed back aboard. The rest were lost.

The bereft *Fleetwing* crossed the finish line at midnight of Christmas Day. *Vesta*, slowed by a navigational error, arrived 40 minutes later. But *Henrietta* had beaten them both. She had swept to victory at 3 p.m. to salvos of applause from the admiring British. Her time: 13 days 21 hours 55 minutes. Her voyage, caroled London's *Daily Telegraph*, was "one of the pluckiest and best pieces of yachting ever seen."

Riding a brisk northwesterly, the big schooners (from right) Vesta, Henrietta and Fleetwing, trailed by more than 200 spectator craft, streak into the Atlantic for the first oceangoing yacht race.

the southern tip of Newfoundland, where the big berg would be sighted the next morning, one of Marshall's guests wrote in his journal: "A beautiful night with a fresh breeze, the ship doing about 12 knots, in an absolutely smooth sea. If it had not been for the temperature (42°) everybody would have stayed on deck for a long time, but warm blankets appealed very strongly and about midnight all went below." All, of course, except Charlie Barr and the hard-working professional crew members on watch, who remained above, shivering in the cold.

But Barr knew how to treat a faithful crew; on May 24 he issued a double allowance of grog to each man to celebrate a sprint of 341 miles in the course of a single day. Since the first night out, *Atlantic* had not sighted any of her competitors, and now everyone aboard began to realize that the schooner was far ahead of the fleet and that she might even break *Endymion's* record. Two days later the winds were at full gale force, and Barr ordered oil bags over the windward side so that their viscous, slow-leaking liquid would smooth the cresting seas. *Atlantic* continued to roar along at 12 knots, with two helmsmen lashed to the wheel to keep them from being washed overboard. That night Marshall's guests, instead of enjoying the view from the deck, stayed in their cabins and prayed. On May 28 the navigator placed *Atlantic* 16½ hours ahead of *Endymion's* pace of five years earlier.

For one more day the winds held strong. Barr kept his course, and *Atlantic* raced past Bishop Rock, only 50 miles from the Lizard. Then the wind began to die. But Barr kept the great yacht moving, and she crossed the finish line, marked by a cruiser from the Imperial German Navy, at 9:16 p.m. Greenwich mean time on May 29, nearly 24 hours ahead of the

Off Sandy Hook, New Jersey, at the start of the 1905 race to England, smoke from the race committee's cannon envelops the schooner Utowana, which, along with the big square-rigged Valhalla behind her, crossed the line too soon and had to try again. The yawl Ailsa—third in line, partly obscuring Valhalla—takes the lead with a fair start, while the three-masted Atlantic (second from left) moves up fast.

second finisher, *Hamburg*. *Atlantic's* winning time was 12 days 4 hours—16 hours faster than *Endymion's* 1900 passage and a sailing record that was not to be beaten until 1980, 75 years later. The new sport of ocean racing was off to a glorious start.

While the big schooners were racing across the Atlantic, an increasing number of yachtsmen on both sides of the ocean were venturing offshore in smaller boats. One of the most active was 44-year-old Thomas Fleming Day, a salty yachtsman who had become somewhat bored with daytime racing. He also happened to be editor of *The Rudder* magazine, in whose pages he continually propagandized for an ocean race. In 1904 Day succeeded in organizing a coastal race from Brooklyn, around New York's Long Island, to Marblehead, Massachusetts, for yachts under 30 feet. Six boats were entered, one of them Day's 25-foot yawl *Sea Bird;* she finished last. The next year, Day organized a second race in the opposite direction, from Brooklyn to Hampton Roads, Virginia. Twice as many yachts entered; this time Day won. He now challenged his readers to participate in a 660-mile contest, from New York to Bermuda.

Only three yachts came out to the starting line off Brooklyn's Gravesend Bay on May 26, 1906: Day's 38-foot yawl *Tamerlane,* Richard Floyd's 40-foot yawl *Lila* and George W. Robinson's 28-foot sloop *Gauntlet.* Less than six hours into the race a squall dismasted *Lila*. In the hazy overcast preceding the storm, *Gauntlet* had taken an early lead; her skipper did not see what happened to *Lila* and he went on his way. But Day was closer to *Lila* and immediately took his *Tamerlane* over to the rescue, shepherding *Lila* back to Gravesend. He was more than two days behind *Gauntlet* when he set out again for Bermuda.

The sumptuous inner sanctum of American yachting

For most of a century the rules and usages of American racing have been handed down from a seven-story limestone palace in midtown Manhattan, headquarters of the New York Yacht Club. Here the country's oldest yachting establishment sets handicap ratings and sponsors scores of races—including the America's Cup. Fittingly, the clubhouse's architecture and decor are at once magisterial and nautical.

Founded in 1844, the club was run from a succession of makeshift apartments for almost 50 years. In 1898 the commodore, financier J. Pierpont Morgan, donated a site just off Fifth Avenue, and three years later the present structure was completed, at a cost of $350,000. As these 1901 photographs show, the clubhouse's architect sprinkled it with enough salt to make the members feel at home—carved marble surf rolling up the balustrades of the grand staircase, sea serpents entwined across mantelpieces, ships' sterns sailing into the façade.

The club's new quarters suited its growing influence. Royalty stopped in for lavish receptions. Edward VII donated a cup. The club also constructed 11 shore stations in the New York area, where members could anchor when sailing. Today the stations have been replaced by a system of guest privileges at other clubs, and the New York Yacht Club sits high and dry, without a dock of its own—a lack that has in no way reduced its prestige as American yachting's most authoritative body.

The baronial richness of the Model Room—4,370 square feet of oak-paneled, Tiffany-glassed exuberance—all but overwhelms its main exhibit: hundreds of boat models that trace the evolution of yacht design from 1844. The black-hulled America *sits atop a glass case in front of the carved Italian stone mantelpiece.*

The club's massive façade, an official New York City landmark, is a nautically inspired hodgepodge of ornamental stonework. The three small bays set into the main-floor windows at left are carved to represent the stern lights of Dutch "jachts" of the 17th Century.

The Grill Room, with curved beams and light fixtures that resemble ships' lanterns, was designed to convince members that they are dining between decks on an 18th Century man-of-war—though the fare served there has never been spartan.

Luck favored the good Samaritan. Far in the lead, *Gauntlet* encountered a southeast gale while crossing the Gulf Stream and had to run off to the northwest for more than 48 hours. Meanwhile, Day was making up lost time. The storm had moderated by the time his *Tamerlane* crossed the Gulf Stream, and Day raced on to beat *Gauntlet* into Bermuda's Hamilton harbor. Poor *Lila*, rejoining the race three days late, ran into a new set of squalls that threatened to topple her rerigged mast, and skipper Floyd had to turn back a second time.

It was an inauspicious start for an ocean-racing series. But the determined Day refused to give up and continued to promote his brain child in the pages of *The Rudder*. A dozen yachts showed up for the start of the second Bermuda race the following year, including a completely overhauled *Lila*. The contestants were divided into two classes, and *Lila* won the trophy for boats under 50 feet. Still, even Day's continuing enthusiasm failed to sustain the interest of many yachtsmen. The number of Bermuda race entries dwindled in succeeding years, and World War I brought the contest to a halt.

Not until 1922 was the Bermuda race revived, and then by another

The schooner Atlantic, running under shortened headsails and a double-reefed foresail and main, battles a three-day gale in the 1905 Kaiser's Cup transatlantic race. When her anxious owner ordered the skipper, the redoubtable Charlie Barr, to heave to, the reply was polite but firm. "Sir, you hired me to win this race," the Scotsman declared, "and that is what I'm trying to do."

yachting journalist. Herbert L. Stone, editor of *Yachting* magazine—*Rudder*'s strongest competitor—persuaded his publishers to put up a silver cup for the event. And like Day before him, Stone urged his readers to take up the challenge of the open-ocean run to Bermuda. The race, he declared, would "develop in the amateur sailor a love of true seamanship and the art of navigation."

Stone's appeal was more successful than Day's had been. No fewer than 23 yachts were at the starting line at Sarah's Ledge off New London, Connecticut, on June 12, 1923. This race was notable for the performance of a new type of yacht that was perfectly suited for ocean racing: the Alden schooner, designed and built by New England yachtsman John Alden. Patterned on the famous, sturdy fishing schooners of Gloucester, Massachusetts, Alden's schooners were eminently seaworthy—and fast. Three of them finished among the top five in their class, with Alden's own *Malabar IV* the winner.

The 1923 contest assured the popularity of the Alden schooner, but the Bermuda race did not immediately capture the imagination of most American yachtsmen. Next year the entry list dwindled to 14, whereupon Stone made a decision that rescued the race from what appeared to be imminent oblivion. Concluding that once a year was too often for racing yachtsmen to get their boats and crews in proper condition for an open-ocean contest, Stone proposed that the Bermuda race be made a biennial event. Sixteen yachts showed up for the 1926 race, 24 in 1928 and an imposing flotilla of 42—many of them Alden schooners or copies—for the race in 1930.

The Bermuda race survived the Depression of the 1930s, despite some frightening and freakish accidents. During the 1932 race, the schooner *Adriana* caught fire at night (page 153); her crew was rescued because, luckily, a British yacht happened to be within sight of her distress signal and her flaming sails. Still, one man drowned. In the same race, the ketch *Curlew*'s navigator became so confused that he instructed the helmsman to sail 45° off course. *Curlew* and her befuddled crew were finally located by a dirigible near Nantucket Shoals, 100 miles northeast of the rest of the racing fleet.

American offshore racing during these decades was not confined to the dash to Bermuda. The race across the Pacific from California to Hawaii—or Transpac as it became known—was born the same year as Thomas Day's Bermuda race, 1906. Though it covered nearly 2,300 miles—five times as much open ocean as its Atlantic counterpart—it often was less hazardous. Once out on the Pacific, unless faced with a rare storm, a skipper had only to settle back and let the northeast trade winds take him on a straight southwesterly course to Diamond Head.

One veteran of the Honolulu race wrote: "All good navigators are agreed that the passage to the Hawaiian Islands offers the simplest job in this line that you can tackle anywhere in the world. There is fine weather all the way, the sun is most obliging and allows you to shoot him to your heart's content, especially near the islands. The seas are never what can really be called heavy. Fog is a rare visitor. The islands are high and plastered with lighthouses, while the reefs extend only a short distance from the shore. The group of islands presents a target 210 miles in width for you to shoot at (unlike the tiny Bermudas) and some of them are visible over 100 miles away."

Between 1906 and 1936 the Transpac was staged 10 times. In 1936, it was scheduled as a biennial event to be held in odd-numbered years, alternating with the Bermuda race, which was sailed in even years.

Conservative British yachtsmen had been slow to follow suit with an ocean race of their own. Hundreds of American and a few British yachtsmen were sailing in regularly scheduled American offshore competitions by 1925, when the first British ocean race was inaugurated. The event was called the Fastnet, because the course ran from the Isle of Wight down the Channel and across part of the Atlantic to the lighthouse on Fastnet Rock off the southwestern Irish coast, before returning to Plymouth in the Channel.

Some transocean veterans at first considered the Fastnet race less challenging than the sail to Bermuda or Hawaii. Only about 175 miles of its course, the stretch of the Atlantic just south of the Irish Sea, could be called open ocean. But those who entered the race quickly discovered what English fishermen had known for centuries: The waters along the 615-mile Fastnet course presented a full ration of hazards. Navigating the obstacle course of shoals, lee shores and fierce tidal currents of the English Channel was a tough test of seamanship for any sailor; and the ocean between England and Ireland, when stirred by a gale, was potentially one of the roughest stretches of water on the face of the earth.

Only seven yachts started the first Fastnet race on August 15, 1925. The winner was *Jolie Brise*, a 56-foot converted Le Havre pilot cutter that ghosted through calms and fog to finish in 6 days 2 hours 45 minutes. Not so lucky were the trailing boats, which got caught in a gale near the end of the race and were forced to run for shelter. All eventually made it to safety, but their rough treatment was a foretaste of the perils that the Fastnet race would offer future contestants.

By the following year, 1926, the Fastnet had become an international competition, attracting an American contender—an Alden schooner— *Primrose IV*, in addition to eight British yachts. Once again the slower boats were caught by a gale, and the 50-foot *Gull* nearly became the Fastnet's first victim.

The owner and skipper of *Gull* was an Irish lawyer; his amateur crew included an American, Warwick Tompkins, who described his companions as "a pack of wild Irishmen who flogged the life out of her." Running into the gale after rounding Fastnet Rock, *Gull* was pounded by a heavy cross sea, losing most of the calking in her bow. Almost immediately water started rising above the floorboards. With the seas breaking over *Gull's* deck, her captain decided to run the vessel onto the nearest mudbank in Baltimore harbor on the Irish coast, recalk her bow and get back into the race. He made it to a mudbank, but barely. The boat passed within 200 yards of the Stag Rocks; "on the darkest, wildest sort of night," Tompkins recounted, "they were plainly visible and audible, great and terrifying founts of spray just to leeward."

Gull's bow was too badly battered to complete the race. Another small yacht, *Altair*, also was forced to run for shelter. *Ilex*, the winner, nearly

lost a crew member who too nonchalantly grabbed the mainsheet as the big yawl's main boom was swept across the deck by the gusting wind; he dangled over the water until the boom came swinging back and let him drop neatly into the cockpit. The American entry, *Primrose IV*, won second place, but only after her balloon staysail was ripped to ribbons. The lessons of the 1926 race, however, were not enough to dissuade more yachtsmen from entering the 1927 Fastnet, which turned out to be the wildest one so far.

For a week before the start of the third Fastnet the weather had been "utterly disgusting," in the words of *Yachting Monthly*, a British magazine that, accustomed to Channel weather, was not given to hyperbole on the subject. On August 13 the squalls and gales moderated—just long enough for the committee to decide not to postpone the race. The 15 starting yachts had not even worked their way around the Isle of Wight into the English Channel when the winds blew up to gale force again. Even before reaching the open ocean the racing fleet was battling a deadly combination of howling winds, nasty seas, and foul tides. Large and small yachts were inundated, battered and driven off course. Nine yachts never reached the Lizard, only 180 miles from the start. *Altair*, unlucky again, blew out her mainsail and put into Weymouth harbor. The crews of *Nelly* and *Penboch* fought the storms to exhaustion and gave up. *Shira* sprang a leak and turned back. *Spica* wore out her bilge pump. *Thalassa* and *Maitenes* split their sails. *Morwenna* ran for refuge, with an injured crew member.

The square-rigged, 47-foot *Saoirse*, which previously had sailed around the world, fought the Channel head winds for three days, gaining nothing on her course, until a mountainous sea rolled over her and flooded her cabin. Her skipper, Conor O'Brien, reluctantly decided to abandon the course and run for cover. Next day *Saoirse* was back in the sheltered waters of the Solent—where the winds were still blustery enough to drive one local yacht onto *Saoirse*'s bowsprit and cause another to splinter her side.

Out at the Scilly Isles, where the Channel gave way to the open Atlantic, the race had narrowed to a handful of yachts. Aboard his 47-foot cutter *Tally-Ho*, Hugh Grosvenor, Lord Stalbridge, was nearing the Lizard when he saw *Jolie Brise*, the heavy-weather winner of the first Fastnet and a favorite in this one, running for shelter. Stalbridge, a competitive horseman as well as yachtsman, reacted characteristically. "Now was our chance," he wrote later.

He had abiding faith in *Tally-Ho*, which previously had weathered a

The Kaiser's Kiel Week: regatta with an imperial stamp

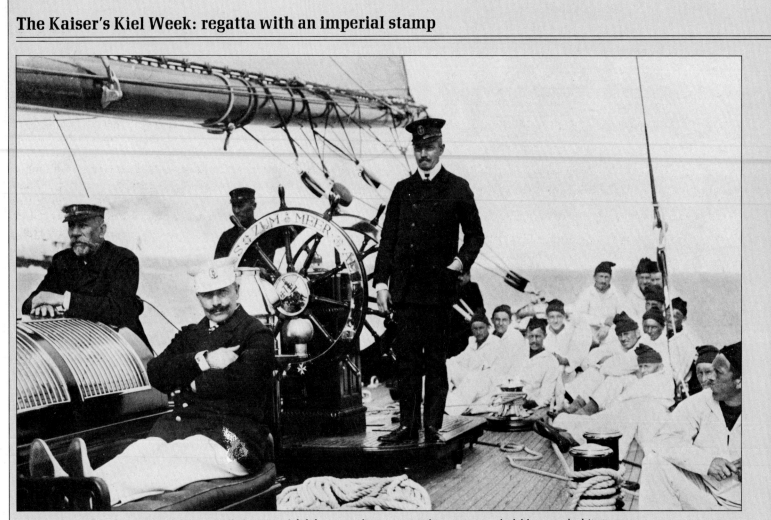

Aboard his new Meteor IV in 1910, Kaiser Wilhelm (seated, left foreground), sports a yachtsman's cap, dark blazer and white trousers.

murderous gale in the Bay of Biscay. But before sticking the yacht's nose out into the ocean, Stalbridge hove to, double-reefed the main, reefed the foresail and exchanged the jib for a small, heavy-duty storm jib. He also lashed canvas covers over all hatches and skylights and trussed down the dinghy, spare spars and anything else that might come loose. As *Tally-Ho's* crew made ready, the 58-foot Alden-designed schooner *Nicanor*, one of two American entries, came plunging back toward the mainland for shelter. At about the same time, Stalbridge was surprised to see another British yacht, *Ilex*, winner of the 1926 race, fly past him, heading for the open ocean. But even before *Tally-Ho* was completely battened down, *Ilex* came floundering back for cover, her headsails blown to ribbons and her mainsail already doused and furled.

Tally-Ho inched out into the tempest, taking the full force of the winds and seas. She climbed skyward on each swell, then surfed down its slope. One enormous wave stopped her in her tracks, shook her hull and sent spray higher than her mainsail. Stalbridge was not encouraged

---

"The Germans are not a yachting nation," Prince Henry of Prussia confided to an English friend in 1909. "Our people race yachts to please my brother. I dare say they get very seasick." He was exaggerating, of course. Not all German yachtsmen had taken up the sport just because his brother, the Kaiser, wanted them to. But it did sometimes seem that Kaiser Wilhelm II was imposing yachting on Germany by the sheer force of his imperial will.

Wilhelm, an impetuous, overbearing autocrat, was determined to make Germany a leading maritime power. This, he believed, meant building not only a strong navy, but also a tradition of competitive sailing. He set an example by taking up sailing himself.

When he came to the throne in 1888, no one in Germany knew how to design or construct a large racing yacht. Wilhelm's first boat was the Scottish-built *Thistle*, at one time an America's Cup contender, which he purchased in 1892 and renamed *Meteor*. For lack of trained German deck hands, he had to employ an English captain and crew. He continued to order his yachts from abroad until 1909. By that year the

boatbuilders in his country had finally learned enough to provide him with *Meteor IV*, a grand 129-foot schooner *(opposite)*, which by then could be manned by Germans.

In 1891 Wilhelm founded the Imperial Yacht Club at Kiel, a seaport on the Baltic, and named himself commodore. Each June he moved in with his court, all bedecked in blazers, brass buttons and yachting caps, for a week or more of rigorously organized racing. Kiel Week, he resolved, would outshine Cowes Week as the premier international yachting event in Europe. The contests included a 300-mile race across the North Sea from Dover to the German island of Helgoland.

Wilhelm did not personally compete in the Helgoland race. "The Kaiser's very fond of giving these 'ere long races, but he takes precious good care he don't sail in 'em himself," remarked one English skipper. Instead, the Emperor waited out the contest aboard his 4,000-ton steamer, the *Hohenzollern*, leading his dutiful staff in morning calisthenics on the fantail.

Kiel Week soon attracted a large number of foreign visitors. Whatever

the regatta in the relatively sheltered Baltic may have lacked in competitive edge, it made up for in flamboyance. There were brass bands and parades, award ceremonies aboard the *Hohenzollern*, receptions at the local *Schloss* and, said one visitor, "an astonishing amount of heel clicking and saluting." The regatta displayed a strong military stamp, in fact, as did everything else to which the Kaiser turned his hand. When sailing aboard one of his *Meteors*, for example, he was invariably attended by an escort of gunboats.

As the Kaiser's reign advanced, the military presence at Kiel took an ominous turn. By 1913 the yachts in the harbor were all but overrun by squadrons of dreadnoughts, U-boats and destroyers. Then, in 1914, the regatta was cancelled—swept aside by the opening blasts of World War I.

By the time the meet resumed after the War, the imperial fanfare that had marked its beginning had vanished. Germany was a republic and Wilhelm an exile, but the Kaiser had achieved at least one of his aims: The Germans at last had a tradition of yacht racing—only now they did it for the fun of it.

when he saw a big oil tanker nearby, plunging up and over the high waves, the keel beneath her bow exposed as she rose, and her propeller and most of her rudder out of the water as she fell. He decided to wait a little longer to see if the storm would moderate. *Tally-Ho* scooted back into the lee of Newlyn harbor.

By 6 a.m. the wind did seem a bit lighter, and by 6:30 *Tally-Ho* was again on her way toward Fastnet Rock. Off Land's End a mountainous sea was still running. Not another vessel was in sight. After a few punishing hours of beating into the gale, *Tally-Ho* found the going easier as the wind hauled into the southwest and abated a little. Able now to lay a straight line for Fastnet, Stalbridge sailed through "a fine night." At dawn there was a sail astern.

Stalbridge recognized the distinctive silhouette of the trailing yacht. She was an Alden schooner, the 54-foot *La Goleta* (Spanish for "the schooner"), owned by American yachtsman Ralph Peverley. Stalbridge was encouraged to see that the bigger American yacht was astern of him, since, under the Fastnet handicap rules, the shorter *Tally-Ho* held a time allowance of nearly five hours over the American. Although neither skipper knew it, theirs were the only yachts left in the race. Throughout the day the barometer was dropping and rain nearly hid them from each other as *La Goleta* closed the gap to only a mile. A pitch-black night had fallen when the yachts approached Fastnet lighthouse. Then the wind died altogether. The two vessels were in the eye of the gale.

Sails slatting, the yachts rolled in the swells pulsing toward the rock-bound Irish coast, which was all the more threatening for being invisible in the darkness. During the next three hours, both skippers managed to use the currents—and a frail land breeze—to maneuver around the high, winking light. As the boats pointed their bows eastward for the homeward voyage, *La Goleta* was a quarter of a mile astern of *Tally-Ho*. Then, suddenly, the storm burst over them again.

The wind came from the northeast, against the northward-moving waves, and kicked up a vicious cross sea. Had either skipper been on a casual cruise, he would have run for the nearest port. Instead, each kept racing for two more hours, unreefed sails thrumming in the steadily increasing wind. Not until the gusts reached 60 miles an hour did they finally shorten down, Stalbridge taking reefs in all his sails and Peverley dousing all canvas except his foresail and forestaysail. The two yachts now drove along at nine knots, *La Goleta* still chasing *Tally-Ho* through the thundering night.

The American yachtsman-journalist Alfred Loomis was racing as co-navigator aboard *La Goleta*. He suggested to Peverley the possibility of quitting. Retiring from a race when a win appeared impossible was an accepted custom among British yachtsmen. Even discounting her time allowance, *Tally-Ho* was in the lead. Moreover, the British cutter was a better heavy-weather boat than *La Goleta*, and Stalbridge would be likely to increase his lead in this storm. But *La Goleta's* other navigator, a British naval officer named John Boyd, argued that they could expect diminishing winds, which would be better schooner weather, and Peverley decided to keep going.

Boyd turned out to be mistaken. The winds rose to 50 miles an hour. *La*

In England's first ocean race, the husky, bluff-bowed Jolie Brise rounds Fastnet Light under gloomy skies during the evening of August 19, 1925. A converted Le Havre pilot cutter of 56 feet, Jolie Brise sped home at the head of the fleet. She went on to win two more Fastnet races, in 1928 and 1930.

Goleta heeled until her cabintop was awash. Peverley struck all canvas except the foresail and forestaysail. *La Goleta* still plunged along at nine knots, as the men who were standing deck watch cringed under the stinging rain. Not until dawn did the wind begin to slacken and haul around to the northwest. Finally *La Goleta* blossomed with all sail set, and took off after *Tally-Ho.*

That same morning crewman Bill Tallman, who had survived the night on the sea-washed, pitching deck, fell overboard. By sheer luck he caught a line and was pulled back on board, with one sea boot washed off and a sodden cigar still stuck in his teeth.

At four that afternoon, on the long reach home, with the wind off the beam and all sails aloft and straining, *La Goleta* caught up with *Tally-Ho.* By nightfall the schooner had pulled ahead, and the wind was piping up again. Through the better part of another crashing night, Peverley kept *La Goleta's* sails flying—ordering the big balloon jib lowered only when her bowsprit started plunging into the sea. With the waves snatching at their heels, *La Goleta's* foredeck hands managed to get the big jib down without being washed overboard. The schooner scarcely slowed. The wind was now astern, and the swells rolled her nearly out of control as they passed under her keel. Terrifyingly, with each long, slow roll the big main boom threatened to jibe over and send the yacht broaching to the white-capped seas. All night Peverley and two expert helmsmen spelled one another at the wheel, grimly holding course.

It was after midnight when *La Goleta* made her landfall and went shooting through the crosscurrents of Runnelstone into the Channel. In the lee of the English coast, Peverley sent *La Goleta* skimming over the smoother water at eight knots, running flat out for the finish line off Drake's Island at the mouth of Plymouth harbor.

But it was not enough. *La Goleta's* lead was too small. She crossed the finish line only 42 minutes ahead of *Tally-Ho*, not enough to make up for the British yacht's time allowance. As *Tally-Ho* came into Plymouth harbor, *La Goleta* sailed alongside her to salute her crew with three polite cheers. Aboard *Tally-Ho*, Lord Stalbridge and his crew emerged from the cabin, all bathed, shaved and neatly dressed as if they had just finished a pleasure cruise.

The successes of the Bermuda and Fastnet races kindled renewed interest among yachtsmen in racing all the way across the Atlantic. There had not been such a contest since *Atlantic's* 1905 Kaiser's Cup victory. By now the Kaiser was out of power, but another European monarch stepped forward as a sponsor. Early in 1928 Spain's King Alfonso XIII, a dedicated amateur sailor, announced a transatlantic race to be sailed from New York to Santander, Spain. Alfonso offered a silver cup for large yachts, and his wife, Queen Victoria, added a cup of her own for smaller boats. This combined contest for the King's and Queen's Cups became an important milestone in offshore competition because it marked the introduction of a new type of ocean-racing yacht.

Two United States businessmen, Paul Hammond and Elihu Root Jr., commissioned W. Starling Burgess—the genius who later produced three America's Cup defenders, including the great J-boat *Ranger*—to design a yacht specifically for the race to Spain. She was to be named after Columbus' favorite ship, *Niña*. Because of the varying sizes of the entries in each class, the race would be run under handicap rules, and Burgess came up with a schooner whose measurements were tailored to make the most of the handicapping system adopted for the race. He perceived, for example, that the rules placed an excessive penalty on narrow hulls and a premium on a deep draft. Therefore, he bestowed on the 59-foot *Niña* a beamy hull more than 15 feet wide and a deep, 9-foot-3-inch keel—neither of which seriously hampered her seagoing performance but both of which combined to give her an enviable time allowance. She thus gained an advantage, for instance, even over a smaller competitor, *Pinta* (actually Fastnet veteran *Nicanor*, which had been renamed for the race to Spain). Although *Pinta* was two feet shorter than *Niña*, her narrower hull meant she would have to finish 10 hours 21 minutes ahead of the larger boat in order to win.

Niña's rig was revolutionary for an offshore yacht. Her towering 72-foot mainmast, which was stepped slightly forward of the normal position on a schooner, sported an enormous Marconi mainsail—still something of a novelty in 1928. Her builder, Reuben Bigelow of Buzzards Bay,

A tough old test far from the sea

America's oldest long-distance yacht race—and one of the country's toughest—takes place some 700 miles from the nearest ocean. It is the Chicago-Mackinac race, 333 miles up the length of Lake Michigan and every bit as demanding as its salt-water counterparts.

In 1898, five Chicago yacht owners heading to Mackinac Island, a resort in the straits between Lake Michigan and Lake Huron, decided to see who could get there fastest. The wind was fair, the contest zestful, so in 1904 they tried again. Ten boats raced, and the Chicago Yacht Club put up a $1,500 trophy shaped like an Indian canoe. The Chicago-Mackinac was established.

The annual quest for the Mackinac Cup is a battle against the unexpected. Great Lakes winds can be gentle zephyrs one moment and roaring gales the next. In 1911, eleven boats left Chicago in weather "as peaceful as a sleeping kitten," said one entrant. Then the barometer plunged and the wind gusted to 80 mph. Three yachts took shelter and one large sloop, *Vencedor*, crashed into a reef, luckily without loss of life. Seven boats continued, and the 100-foot schooner *Amorita* ran home in 31 hours 14 minutes, the course record.

Despite such weather, the Chicago-Mackinac has burgeoned. By the late 1970s, with more than 200 entrants competing for 14 awards and trophies, it had become the world's leading fresh-water yacht race.

THE MACKINAC CUP

Massachusetts, who had never before launched anything larger than day-sailing dinghies and single-sailed cat boats, labored four months on *Niña* and did not complete her until days before the start of the race, so her owners did not have much time to test her.

The committee for the King's and Queen's Cups staggered the start so that both large and small yachts would reach the finish line off Santander at about the same time. The small class departed from Gravesend Bay on June 30, 1928, a week before the big boats. At the outset it was a race between *Niña* and *Pinta*, with another yacht, a 60-foot schooner named *Mohawk*, nearly holding her own against them. *Pinta* had better luck at first; her navigator, Alfred Loomis, took her on a southerly slant until the appearance of floating weeds and glimmering Portuguese men-of-war told him that *Pinta* was in the Gulf Stream. Then, with a healthy southwesterly and a strong favorable current, *Pinta* reeled off 253 miles to the east in 24 hours, an unprecedented rate for so small a boat.

But *Niña* was also sprinting eastward. "As the winds were light westerly," wrote her navigator, Laurence Lombard, "this meant driving her with all the light sails we could carry—and we had plenty." In all, Hammond and Root had stocked 26 different sails aboard the new ocean racer. In spite of the tremendous press of canvas, Burgess' tall mast held up even when the winds gusted up to 35 miles an hour, and the schooner maintained a steady pace across the ocean. Then, when the westerlies gave way to headwinds off the continental shelf of Europe, the deep-keeled *Niña* proved herself to be the more weatherly yacht, pointing up better than *Pinta*, overtaking her and going into the lead in full view of *Pinta's* anguished crew.

Drawing nearer to the Spanish waters, the crews of *Niña* and *Pinta* began keeping a lookout for the yachts in the big class, expecting to see them come thundering up from astern at any time. The formidable *Atlantic*, winner of the Kaiser's Cup, would surely be in the lead; at the age of 25 she was still one of the fastest yachts afloat. The giant schooner was now owned by millionaire Gerard Lambert, and at her helm was Charles Francis Adams Jr., America's Cup defender aboard *Resolute* in 1920.

Atlantic overtook *Pinta* near the end of the race, less than 200 miles out from Santander. Both yachts were pointing up into a fresh easterly. The 57-foot *Pinta* was reefed and plunging into head seas that washed over her deck. *Atlantic*, more than three times *Pinta's* length, sliced smoothly through the same waves. Lambert recalled later how he was struck by the contrast. Sitting high and dry on *Atlantic's* afterdeck just before cocktail time, he looked down at *Pinta's* pitching deck and the huddled figures in her wet cockpit and wondered why anyone would willingly suffer such punishment. By the time Lambert went below to inspect the wine the steward had selected for dinner, little *Pinta* was nearly lost in the spray astern.

But *Atlantic* never caught *Niña*. At 2:15 p.m. on July 24, the radically rigged little schooner crossed the finish line off Santander, to be greeted by whistles, rockets and a launch with a man on her cabintop shouting, "Well sailed, *Niña*! I congratulate you! I am the King of Spain."

Niña's performance proved even more than her owners had expected. So fast did she sail on the open ocean that she did not even need her huge

time allowance in order to win the race to Spain. She also proved something else. *Niña's* crewmen—and *Pinta's* as well—were amateurs, unlike the paid hands that were needed aboard the larger, older yachts. In the race to Spain the volunteers aboard the smaller boats worked harder, watch on watch, than paid crews—even dedicated professionals. Gerard Lambert, studying the huddled figures in foul weather gear aboard the spray-washed deck of *Pinta* as he sailed grandly past, did not realize that he was witnessing a yachting revolution. Ocean racing was becoming an amateur sport.

While the race to Spain spelled the end for the big boats, it was the beginning for little *Niña*, whose career would extend for four decades, including a 1962 Bermuda race victory when she was 34 years old. In fact, she scarcely rested in Santander before co-owners Hammond and Root sent her across the Bay of Biscay and up the English Channel to Cowes in time for the 1928 Fastnet race. Most of her transatlantic crew stayed with her. However, Hammond and Root had to return to the United States, and they turned *Niña's* helm over to Sherman Hoyt, the wily America's Cup tactician, who was generally regarded as the best racing sailor in America even then—six years before he steered *Rainbow* to a crucial America's Cup victory over *Endeavour*.

Hoyt, who had spent most of the summer day-racing in Scandinavian waters, arrived at Cowes only two days before the start of the Fastnet race. Stepping aboard *Niña* for the first time, he found her unconventional rig with its dozens of sails unfamiliar and complicated. He selected the canvas he wanted and put ashore "a vast assortment of sail and gear which I considered unessential for Fastnet."

The start of the race, on August 15, 1928, did not favor the American schooner. The wind was astern for the 12-mile easterly run round the Isle of Wight before the yachts headed down the Channel. A dozen vessels, spinnakers bellying, crossed the line at 11:30 a.m., and the larger boats quickly came to the fore. By the time the yachts were halfway to the turn at the eastern tip of the Isle of Wight, *Niña* was in seventh place.

Hoyt had invited a British yachtsman named Weston Martyr aboard *Niña* for the race. Martyr later recalled that he thought *Niña's* falling behind so soon was a "very dreadful" development. "I turned a troubled face toward our skipper," he said. But Hoyt only "smiled a most tranquil smile and winked. 'Wait a while!' said he. I waited."

Martyr had to wait only until the fleet had rounded the turning point and turned west into the wind. After a hectic period of sail changing, he found *Niña* "sailing at seven knots right into the eye of the wind." Scanning the Channel, he recalled, "incredible as it may seem, there were no competitors there!" With her radical rig, *Niña* was pointing into the wind so much better than the rest of the yachts that she was able to make a nearly straight slant down the Channel while the others were beating across it.

Still, *Niña's* wonderful upwind sailing qualities did not guarantee victory, and the American schooner soon suffered her share of minor misfortunes. When the navigator made his first plotting, he placed *Niña* 40 miles inside the French coastline. The problem was a faulty chronometer, and Hoyt found that he would have to navigate the whole race by

dead reckoning, plotting the course every hour and trying to make allowance for the notoriously unpredictable currents where the Channel entered the open Atlantic.

However, the breezes blew mainly from the west, providing the windward work that favored *Niña*. She was first around Fastnet Rock. On the return leg the wind swung into the south, and Hoyt continued to profit by *Niña's* ability to sail closer to the wind than her competitors could. But soon the breezes became capricious, changing direction and velocity and causing Hoyt to alter course almost constantly. At one point, he wrote later, he "was amused to overhear through the skylight one of our youngsters expatiating at length that he had always been taught that a straight line was the shortest distance between two points and why in hell did the skipper keep sailing all over the lot?"

One result of chasing the wind was that *Niña* fetched the English coast eight miles too far to the north. But a fair tide from the Bristol Channel helped her get quickly back on course. Slipping into the English Channel, she picked up a "snorting strong breeze," as Hoyt happily described it, and went racing toward the finish line at Plymouth. The "snorting

A Royal Spanish Yacht Club committee boat and an amphibious plane from the American battle cruiser Detroit welcome Niña as she arrives off Santander, winning the small-yacht class of the 1928 New York-to-Spain race. The Detroit also sent a barge carrying the U.S. Navy band to pipe Niña into port with The Star-Spangled Banner.

breeze'' quickly mounted to a moderate gale, and by nightfall Hoyt found himself driving at full speed toward an unseen Plymouth breakwater. He claimed later that he was still frantically studying the chart, trying to figure out *Niña*'s position, when a gun sounded from the shore, signaling that the American schooner had crossed the finish line. *Niña* had covered the 615-mile course in 4 days 13 hours 48 minutes, and once again she had not needed her favorable time allowance in order to beat the rest of the fleet.

Niña represented ocean racing's first step toward a specialized, high-performance, offshore yacht. Three years later another American racing yacht with an even more radical rig—the 52-foot yawl *Dorade*, designed by 23-year-old American Olin Stephens—clinched the case for the newer, smaller vessels by beating the bigger boats in a 1931 transatlantic race from Newport to Plymouth and following up with a victory in the Fastnet race the same year. Yacht designers on both sides of the Atlantic went back to their drawing boards to emulate Stephens' wonderful yawl. The revolution was complete. The next three decades saw the development of racing yachts that were even smaller and lighter. Sails woven of synthetic fibers replaced those made of heavier cotton. Hulls were made of fiberglass and rudders of carbon fiber and epoxy.

Interest in the sport grew until, in 1958, more than a hundred yachts

The crew of Niña, weary but jubilant after spending 24 days at sea, poses for a victory portrait with the U.S. Ambassador to Spain, Ogden H. Hammond (center). All hands turned out in slacks and sweaters—except for skipper Paul Hammond (second from left), who was so fond of informality that he was barefoot and wearing shorts even when he met the King of Spain.

entered the Bermuda race—the largest of them only half the size of *Fleur de Lys*, which had been the smallest entry in the 1905 Kaiser's Cup race. After World War II more than a dozen new long-distance ocean races were organized to test yachtsmen's skill and stamina—including the 630-mile Sydney to Hobart race through the gale-swept waters of the southern Pacific Ocean; the 1,200-mile Buenos Aires to Rio de Janiero race in the South Atlantic; and for the truly daring and self-confident yachtsman, a quadrennial singlehanded race across the Atlantic that by 1976 drew 100 contestants. Probably the most grueling test of all was a 27,120-mile Round the World race, first staged in 1973-1974 *(page 168)*.

The growth of offshore racing following World War II inevitably brought with it an increasing number of tragedies in what generally had been a surprisingly safe sport. The first death in an organized ocean race did not occur until 1931, when Colonel C. H. Hudson was swept off *Maitenes II* in the Atlantic during that year's Fastnet contest. Four years later, an American, Robert Ames, was tossed out of the cockpit of his yacht *Hamrah* during a race from Newport, Rhode Island, to Norway. Ames's two sons were also aboard, and one of them instantly dived overboard to rescue their father while the other launched a small dinghy. Then, as *Hamrah's* remaining crew struggled back to windward, a giant wave capsized the dinghy and all three men disappeared. In 1977 in a race off Marseilles, seven French yachtsmen aboard their 35-foot *Airel* disappeared without a trace. Still, ocean racers argued that a total of fewer than 30 fatalities among tens of thousands of sailors over three quarters of a century proved that ocean racing was far safer than might have been expected—until the Fastnet race of 1979.

The fatal element, as in so many disasters at sea, was the capricious weather. For three Fastnet races during the 1970s the winds had been unusually moderate. In fact, some sailors had complained about the lack of strong winds during the 1975 and 1977 races. Lulled by the excellent sailing conditions, an increasing number of yachtsmen were tempted by the Fastnet, until by the summer of 1979 more than 300 boats were entered by owners from 19 countries.

Many of them were small even by modern ocean-racing measurements. After only two yachts had managed to finish the 1927 Fastnet, the race had been limited to vessels with a water line at least 35 feet long. But in the 1950s the Fastnet minimum was lowered to 24 feet, and by 1979 it had been further reduced to 22 feet.

A few of the skippers entering the race were lured as much by the social activities at Cowes as by the race itself. "Buy a boat," proclaimed one hardened Fastnet sailor, "call your card-playing friends, and go in a big-name race." Nor were the regulations for Fastnet races as stringent as for many other ocean races. Safety equipment was inspected on only 54 of the 303 boats entered, and there was no requirement that every contestant carry a heavy-duty storm trysail, a small substitute for a mainsail that is essential for ocean sailing. Neither were members of the crews required to have ocean-sailing experience, as they were in the Bermuda and transpacific races.

Australian and New Zealand participants were surprised that two-

Dorade, shown here on her way to Bermuda in 1932, was, said The Times of London, "the most wonderful little ocean racing yacht ever built." A year earlier the 52-foot yawl had raced to England in just 17 days, two days ahead of her nearest rival, and then had won the Fastnet. The victories earned her crew a ticker-tape parade up Broadway.

way radios were not specified for the Fastnet; in their famous Sydney-Hobart race, radio reports were required twice a day. (Some yachtsmen objected to this rule on the grounds that it unfairly revealed to competitors the position of the leaders.) Participants in the Fastnet were not permitted to use Omega or other sophisticated electronic navigation systems, because the race organizers believed that such navigational aids detracted from the challenge of piloting the offshore course. So, when on Saturday, August 11, a swarming armada of 303 yachts crowded the Solent for the start of the 1979 Fastnet race, some of them were ill-prepared for the ordeal they soon would face.

At first the weather beguilingly cooperated, with a gentle breeze through which the heeling horde beat back and forth to round the Isle of Wight and enter the English Channel. The British Meteorological Office predicted easy sailing weather for the next two days. The weathermen warned, however, that there was a chance that a moderate, Force 7 gale would blow up in the Western Approaches by Monday or Tuesday. The predicted winds could reach 32 to 38 miles an hour—no problem for a seaworthy yacht with an experienced crew.

The gale warnings took note of a low-pressure storm system across the Atlantic near Nova Scotia. It did not seem particularly threatening at the start of the race. If the storm followed a normal course, it would move northeastward or southeastward, missing the course of the race entirely. But instead it moved east, directly toward southern Ireland. Moreover, on Sunday, August 12, another storm appeared to the north, off the coast of Iceland, and meteorologists began to worry that the fronts of these two storm systems might clash—with violent consequences.

Some 2,700 amateur sailors, including more than a few women, were meanwhile working their boats down the English Channel, their main concern being fog banks and commercial ships. By Monday noon the entire fleet was in the open Atlantic, and some of the larger, faster vessels were already preparing to round Fastnet Rock.

By this time the weathermen recognized that the danger of clashing storm systems was imminent. On its regularly scheduled radio forecast for mariners at 12:55 p.m., the Meteorological Office cautiously, perhaps too cautiously, upgraded the predicted gale from Force 7 to Force 8 (winds of 39 to 46 miles per hour). Four hours later, concerned about rapidly deteriorating weather conditions, the Meteorological Office broadcast a special warning: A Force 9 gale (winds 47 to 54 mph) was forecast, with a strong probability of Force 10 (winds 55 to 63 mph). This would have been enough to send some prudent skippers running for shelter. But since it was not a scheduled broadcast, most of the Fastnet contestants did not hear it. By 1 a.m. Tuesday, the weather broadcast carried the direst warning of all: Force 10, a whole gale, with winds up to 63 miles an hour. But by that time the yachtsmen did not need any warning of the gale. They were in it.

The storm system from the west had picked up speed and intensified as it headed straight for the waters between England and Ireland. Monday night its front had clashed head on with that of the more northerly storm. At Hartland Point, north of Cornwall, gusts were registered at 85 mph—hurricane force. In the Atlantic south of Ireland, the wind-driven

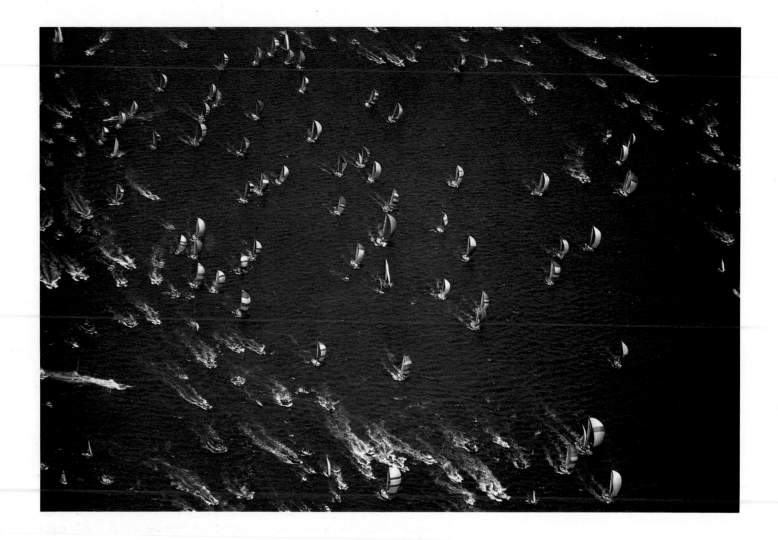

waters piled up into mountainous waves. From atop his tower on Fastnet Rock, the lighthouse keeper looked out on a white, frothing seascape unlike anything he had ever seen except during the worst winter storms. In the many coves along the Irish and Welsh coasts, fishermen snugged down their boats and doubled their mooring lines against the rising winds. But most of the vessels in the Fastnet race had been caught about 100 miles offshore.

Yachtsmen who had raced for decades and had sailed around the world said they had never seen anything like it. The gusts smashed their wind-speed indicators. The rain stung like shotgun pellets. The short, high seas did not simply break at the top as they normally would in mid-ocean, but resembled curling beach surf. It became impossible to ride up the face of such a wave; as it pitched over, it swept and smothered anything in its path.

For the first few hours of the tempest on Monday evening, some of the skippers continued to race, thereby increasing their peril by carrying too much sail. Throughout the night the seas continued to build, smashing across the decks and cockpits and drenching the sailors. In the darkness, phosphorescence gleamed and flickered on foul-weather gear as

Spinnakers billowing, some of a fleet of 67 entrants run down Sydney Harbor in 1967 for the start of the annual race to Hobart, Tasmania. Most yachtsmen think the 630-mile Sydney-Hobart race is the roughest in the world. Its course runs through the roaring forties—the wild westerlies that circle the globe in the high Southern latitudes—and contestants have often been beset by gales, wracking cross seas and even schools of whales.

the yachtsmen struggled to keep their boats on course. Some skippers managed to strip down to storm trysail and heave to, the helmsmen threading their way between the rolling hills of water. But many of the yachts carried no storm trysail.

Many of the biggest boats, which were up to 79 feet long and manned largely by experienced crews, had worked their way into the lead and had rounded Fastnet Rock before the worst of the storm struck on Monday night. But even they were subjected to moments of terror. After rounding the Rock, the 64-foot *Boomerang*, now running under reduced sail, pitched over the brink of a huge wave and raced so fast down its frothing face that her speed indicator registered 24 knots, faster than any clipper-ship record. The powerful gust that pushed *Boomerang* over the wave top registered on her anemometer at an unbelievable 100 knots—115 miles an hour.

As the seas mounted to heights of 40 to 50 feet, many smaller yachts literally fell off the crests as if off ledges, crashing into the troughs between waves, where they were then knocked over and buried by plunging walls of foam that tore their masts from their steps. Some turned turtle, spinning through a full 360 degrees, resurfacing with their cabins full of water.

George Tinley, the English skipper of the 34-foot *Windswept*, elected to douse all sail and put out a sea anchor that had been hastily made of stuffed sail bags shortly after the gale struck. Everyone went below to ride out the storm. *Windswept* seemed to be rolling safely if violently with the seas, when one monster wave picked her up like a wood chip and flipped her over. The cabin lights went out. Everyone was dumped upside down. One man was flung from the main cabin into the forward compartment. The yacht seemed to hang there, keel up and mast down, with the water gushing through her companionway and her crew standing on the ceiling. One of the crew called out, "Never mind, it will come up again in a minute."

The weight of *Windswept's* keel slowly righted the yacht. Her floorboards floated in a wash of sea water along with food cans, tangled gear and sewage that had backed up from the toilet waste pipe. Skipper Tinley was unconscious, his nose and wrist broken. Climbing on deck, the crewmen found the mast broken off and the uninflated life raft over the side, at the end of its towline. They hauled the life raft in, but discovered that it would not inflate; they had no choice but to stay with the yacht. Finding the bilge pumps clogged by debris, they bailed out much of the water by hand. Then, with no sails to help them, they managed to maneuver *Windswept's* stern into the wind by means of the rudder alone. Holding her in that position, they rode out the storm until the winds diminished enough for them to put up a jury rig and limp into Crosshaven, on the south coast of Ireland. Skipper Tinley meanwhile came to and found himself in the cockpit. No one could remember who had brought him up from the flooded cabin.

Thirty-four-foot *Charioteer* did not turn turtle, but she was knocked so far over that her mast went under water—six times. During the sixth knockdown the mast was snapped off and her stove was wrenched from its fittings. It flew across the cabin and struck the skipper, J. B. Coldrey,

The longest long-distance race of them all

On the 8th of September, 1973, seventeen yachts set out from Portsmouth, England, to compete in the most ambitious contest for fully crewed ocean racers since the birth of the sport. In the Whitbread race—named for the British brewery sponsoring it—they would sail around the world, crossing three oceans, touching at three continents and skirting the ice floes of Antarctica—a staggering 27,120 miles.

The yachts, handicapped according to size, ranged from Poland's 45-foot *Copernicus* to Great Britain's 80-foot *Burton Cutter*, and the boats' crews represented an equally broad spread of racing philosophy. A former paratrooper named Chay Blyth, who had once crossed the Atlantic in a rowboat, manned his 77-foot *Great Britain II* with paratroopers on loan from the British Army and maintained spartan discipline. Mexican industrialist Ra-

mon Carlin, on the other hand, took along his family and stocked his 65-foot *Sayula II* with vodka for their afternoon cocktails.

The first leg, from Portsmouth to Cape Town, South Africa, proved to be a shakedown. The crew of the newly launched *Burton Cutter* was still bolting on her fittings as the race began, and France's *Pen Duick IV* lost her mainmast in the first strong breeze. The sparsely provisioned *Great Britain II* ran low on her rations, while *Sayula II* ran out of wine and was down to only 24 jars of caviar by the time she reached Cape Town.

The second leg, 6,600 miles from Cape Town to Sydney, Australia, was a sterner test: perpetual westerlies that roared at 46 mph, and towering seas. Several boats were somersaulted by rogue waves, and an Englishman and a Frenchman were swept off their yachts

and lost. Leg three was just as bad—8,370 storm-tossed miles around Cape Horn to Rio de Janeiro. One of Blyth's paratroopers was lost when he fell overboard into the near freezing waters. The final leg of 5,500 miles back to Portsmouth was marred only by minor accidents.

Great Britain II crossed the line first, on April 11, 1974, after 144 days at sea. Three weeks passed before the last vessel, *Copernicus*, turned up. But the big surprise was the happy-go-lucky *Sayula II*, which sailed nonchalantly into Portsmouth on April 14. She was the sixth to finish, but when her handicap was taken into account she had won the world's longest yacht race.

France's Kriter rounds Cape Horn, through the treacherous currents of one of the world's most dangerous sea passages. She finished in 3,758 hours of sailing time, to take fourth place.

breaking a vertebra in his neck. When *Charioteer* staggered upright, a crewman sighted and signaled a French fishing trawler that was running for cover. The trawler came rolling alongside long enough to pick up the injured Coldrey and his crew.

Some yachtsmen who abandoned their vessels in despair soon had cause to regret taking to their life rafts. Many were thrown out of the pitching rafts repeatedly and eventually became too weak to climb back in. Some hung on for their lives; others drowned. Several rafts came apart in the heavy seas. During Monday night British yachtsman Simon Fleming and seven crewmen from the 37-foot *Trophy* crowded into one life raft, which went bucking off across 40-foot-high waves. The first four times that the raft was overturned, all eight men managed to climb back aboard. The fifth time, two men were washed away. Then the raft split in two. Both sections stayed afloat; Fleming squirmed onto one piece of the raft, his companions onto the other. One of them died of exposure before help finally came with the dawn.

By that time a massive rescue operation was under way, with vessels from the Royal Navy pitching alongside the yachts and Royal Air Force helicopters hovering overhead, reeling down lines to pick up survivors from their rafts. Many of the yachts, awash and abandoned, withstood the storm and were salvaged later. Three men died after they left the 35-foot *Ariadne*, whose mastless hull was found during the rescue operation; whether or not they could have survived aboard the battered yacht was an open question. In all, 15 yachtsmen died—by far the greatest number of deaths in a single event in the 300-year history of yacht racing. All of those who lost their lives were in the three smallest classes of yachts—none longer than 38 feet overall—only 13 of which managed to complete the course.

The tragedy of the 1979 Fastnet led to a thorough study of the race by a committee from the Royal Yachting Association and the Royal Ocean Racing Club. The investigation included a lengthy questionnaire that was sent to survivors. Seventy per cent of the respondents estimated maximum wind speed at Force 11—64 to 75 miles an hour—or above, and 33 per cent said their boats had been knocked so far over that their masts were below the horizontal. No fewer than 23 yachts were abandoned by their crews.

Although the storm had all too clearly revealed the shortcomings of some of the boats and their crews and equipment, it had also demonstrated that a well-found, ably sailed yacht could weather the worst that nature has to offer. Of the starting fleet of 303 vessels, 85 made it safely to the finish line. The winner was the 61-foot sloop *Tenacious*, owned and skippered by the thoroughly competent United States yachtsman Ted Turner, who had successfully defended the America's Cup two years earlier. He and his crew were so confident in their own performance and that of their yacht, said Turner, that at the height of the storm they enjoyed a steak dinner. And, in a nostalgic coincidence, the 66-year-old but still-sturdy cutter *Jolie Brise*—winner of the very first Fastnet race and two later ones, and now owned by the Exeter, England, Maritime Museum—came romping home through the storm from a cruise to Portugal, with no damage and no injury to anyone aboard.

A helicopter swings into position to rescue the last waiting crewman from the 34-foot English sloop Camargue *during the storm that took 15 lives in the 1979*

Fastnet race. The yacht's tall mast prevented the helicopter from plucking survivors from her deck, so the eight men jumped into the water to be picked up.

Acknowledgments

The index for this book was prepared by Gale Linck Partoyan. The editors wish to thank the following: John Batchelor, artist, and William A. Baker and Halsey Herreshoff, consultants (pages 90-95 and 108-111); Peter McGinn, artist (endpaper maps); Richard Schlecht, artist, and Arthur Knapp Jr., Vice President, Ratsey & Lapthorn, Inc., Sailmakers, and Roderick Stephens, Vice President, Sparkman & Stephens, Naval Architects, consultants (pages 120-125).

The editors also wish to thank: In Bermuda: Hamilton—Diana Darby, The Bermuda Publishing Company. In France: Paris—Philippe Henrat, Curator, Archives Nationales; Claude J. Breguet; Michel Etevenon; Hervé Cras, Director for Historical Studies, Jacques Chantriot, Denise Chaussegroux, Catherine Touny, Researchers, Musée de la Marine; Érwan Quémeré; Hubert de Saint-Senoch; Yacht Club de France; Saint-Hilaire du Harscouët—Marin Marie. In Germany: Bremerhaven—Arnold Kludas, Deutsches Schiffahrtsmuseum; Hamburg—Dr. Jürgen Meyer, Altonaer Museum; Kiel—Dr. Jürgen Jensen, Stadtarchiv; Admiral Hans-Rudolf Rösing. In Italy: Genoa—Beppe Croce, President, Yachting Club Italiano. In Spain: Madrid—Trini Bandres; Peter Debelius; Santander—Don Alfonso Suárez, Head Archivist to the Ayuntamiento, Elina Salcedo, Secretary to the Ayuntamiento. In Sweden: Stockholm—Dr. Gösta Webe, Curator, Statens Sjöhistoriska Museum. In the

United Kingdom: London—Marjorie Willis, BBC Hulton Picture Library; Linda Gilliam, Cruising Association; Elizabeth Moore, Illustrated London News Picture Library; Jane Dacy, Picture Department, Esme Greenslade, Library, Joan Moore, Photographic Department, National Maritime Museum; Bertram Newbury, Parker Gallery; Michael S. Robinson; Elizabeth Hamilton, Royal Ocean Racing Club; E. Hamilton-Parks, Royal Thames Yacht Club; Frank G. G. Carr, World Ship Trust; Alverstoke—Charles B. Blake; Beken—Christine Haines; Cowes—Major J. D. Dillon, Secretary, Spencer Herapath, Royal Yacht Squadron; Glasgow—Rosemary Watt, Glasgow Museum and Art Gallery; Stockbridge—Lieutenant Colonel D. G. St. John Radcliffe; Sir Thomas Sopwith; Adare, Ireland—The Earl and Countess of Dunraven.

The editors also wish to thank: In the United States: Washington, D. C.—Commander Ralph Emerson, British Naval Attache's Office, British Embassy; William Hezlep, Office of the Geographer, United States Department of State; Branford, Connecticut—Charles H. Vilas; Chicago, Illinois—Chicago Historical Society; Samuel Clarke, Librarian, Chicago Yacht Club; Dover, Massachusetts—Charles F. Adams; Hoboken, New Jersey—Jane Hartye, Associate Curator, S. C. Williams Library, Stevens Institute; Larchmont, New York—Clifford H. Wolfe; Marblehead, Massachusetts—Eugene T. Connolly, Mr. and Mrs.

Chester Sawtelle; Mystic, Connecticut—Richard C. Malley, Assistant Registrar, Lisa Halttunen, Reference Librarian, Mystic Seaport Museum; Nashville, Tennessee—Marice Wolfe, Head of Special Collections, Vanderbilt University Library; New Haven, Connecticut—Judith Schiff, Manuscript and Archives Department, Yale University Library; New York, New York—Mrs. Stevens Baird; Mrs. Paul Hammond; Sohei Hohri, Librarian, Frank MacLear, Alexander Salm, New York Yacht Club; Stanley Rosenfeld; Gretchen Wessels; Rosemary Curley, Yachting; Newport, Rhode Island—John Cherol, Curator, The Preservation Society of Newport County; Newport News, Virginia—Paul B. Hensley, Archivist, Larry Gilmore, Charlotte Valentine, Library Assistant, The Mariners Museum; Oklahoma City, Oklahoma—Marjorie Young Burgess Wolff; Salem, Massachusetts—Kathy Flynn, The Peabody Museum; San Francisco, California—John Maounis, Photograph Librarian, National Maritime Museum at San Francisco; Unionville, Pennsylvania—John C. West; Waterbury, Connecticut—D. S. Hibbard, Brass Division, Anaconda Industries.

Valuable sources of quotations were The $30,000,000 Cup: The Stormy History of the Defense of the America's Cup by Jerome E. Brooks, Simon and Schuster, 1958, and Ocean Racing: The Great Blue-Water Yacht Races, 1866-1935 by Alfred F. Loomis, William Morrow and Company, 1936.

Bibliography

Barrault, Jean Michel, Great Moments of Yachting. G. P. Putnam's Sons, 1967.

Bell, Helen G., Winning the King's Cup. G. P. Putnam's Sons, 1928.

Birch, Thomas, The History of the Royal Society. Johnson Reprint Corporation, 1968.

Boswell, Charles, The America: The Story of the World's Most Famous Yacht. David McKay, 1967.

Bradford, Ernle, Three Centuries of Sailing. Country Life, 1964.

Brooks, Jerome E., The $30,000,000 Cup: The Stormy History of the Defense of the America's Cup. Simon and Schuster, 1958.

Burgess, Edward, American and English Yachts. Charles Scribner's Sons, 1887.

Burnell, R. D., Races for the America's Cup. London: Macdonald, 1965.

Carter, Samuel, Boatbuilders of Bristol. Doubleday, 1970.

Chapelle, Howard I., The History of American Sailing Ships. Bonanza Books, 1935.

Clark, Arthur H., The History of Yachting, 1600-1815. G. P. Putnam's Sons, 1904.

Cook, Peter and Bob Fisher, The Longest Race. David McKay, 1975.

Cotter, Edward F., The Offshore Game: Today's Ocean Racing. Crown Publishers, 1977.

Davidson, Kenneth, "Model Tests of Sailing Yachts." The Rudder, August, 1937.

Davis, Murray, Australian Ocean Racing. Sydney: Angus and Roberts, 1967.

Dear, Ian, Enterprise to Endeavour: The J-Class Yachts. Dodd, Mead, 1977.

Drummond, Maldwin, Salt-Water Palaces. Viking, 1979.

Dunlap, G. D., America's Cup Defenders. American Heritage, 1970.

Dunraven, Earl of, Past Times and Pastimes. London: Hodder and Stoughton, 1922.

The Editors of Time-Life Books, Offshore (Library of Boating). Time-Life Books, 1976.

Feversham, Lord Charles, Great Yachts. G. P. Putnam's Sons, 1970.

Fraser, Antonia, Royal Charles: Charles II and the Restoration. Alfred A. Knopf, 1979.

Gavin, Charles M., Royal Yachts. London: Rich and Cowan, 1962.

Grout, Jack, C'Était au Temps des Yachtsmen: Histoire Mondiale du Yachting des Origines a 1939. Paris: Editions Gallimard, 1978.

Guest, Montague and William B. Boulton, The Royal Yacht Squadron. London: John Murray, 1903.

Gurney, Guy, "Fastnet and the Admiral's Cup." Yachting, November, 1979.

Heaton, Peter, Yachting: A History. London: B. T. Batsford, 1955.

Heckstall-Smith, Anthony, Sacred Cowes. London: Allan Wingate, 1955.

Heckstall-Smith, B., All Hands on the Main-Sheet. London: Grant Richards, 1921.

Herapath, Spencer, The Royal Yacht Squadron: 1815-1975. Cowes: Royal Yacht Squadron, 1976.

Herreshoff, L. Francis:
Capt. Nat Herreshoff. Sheridan House, 1953.
An Introduction to Yachting. Sheridan House, 1963.

Hoyt, C. Sherman, Sherman Hoyt's Memoirs. D. Van Nostrand, 1950.

Hughes, John Scott:

Famous Yachts. London: Methuen, 1928.

The Harbours of the Solent. Christopher Johnson Publishers, 1956.

Irving, John, *The King's Britannia.* London: Seeley Service, 1937.

Johnson, Peter, *Ocean Racing and Offshore Yachts.* Dodd, Mead, 1972.

Julyan, Herbert E., *Sixty Years of Yachts.* London: Hutchinson, 1950.

King, Joe, "Design for Speed." *New York World-Telegram,* April 3, 1937.

Kinney, Francis S., *"You Are First," the Story of Olin and Rod Stephens, Inc.* Dodd, Mead, 1978.

Landmarks Preservation Commission (New York) "Designation List #127," September 11, 1979.

Lindsay, Nigel, *The America's Cup.* London: Heath Cranton, 1930.

Lombard, Laurence M., *Log of the Niña in the Race for the Queen of Spain's Cup, July 1-July 24, 1928.*

Loomis, Alfred F., *Ocean Racing: The Great Blue-Water Yacht Races, 1866-1935.* William Morrow, 1936.

McGowan, A. P., *Royal Yachts.* London: Her Majesty's Stationery Office, 1977.

Martyr, Weston, "Niña Wins the Fastnet Race," *Yachting,* October 1928.

Ogg, David, *England in the Reign of Charles II.* Clarendon Press, 1934.

Parkinson, John Jr., *The History of the New York Yacht Club.* 2 vols. The New York Yacht Club, 1975.

Phillips-Birt, Douglas:

British Ocean Racing. London: Adlard Coles, 1960.

The Cumberland Fleet: Two Hundred Years of Yachting 1775-1975. London: The Royal Thames Yacht Club, 1978.

The History of Yachting. Stein and Day, 1974.

Plimpton, George, "The Ultimate Triumph." *Sports Illustrated,* October 29, 1956.

Poor, Charles Lane, *Men against the Rule: A Century of Progress in Yacht Design.* The Derrydale Press, 1937.

Robinson, Bill:

The Great American Yachts Designers. Alfred A. Knopf, 1974.

Legendary Yachts. David McKay, 1978.

Rousmaniere, John, *Fastnet, Force 10.* W. W. Norton, 1980.

Steers, James R., "The Log of the Yacht America." *Yachting,* Part I, December 1946. Part II, January 1947.

Stevenson, Paul E., *The Race for the Emperor's Cup.* The Rudder Publishing Company, 1907.

Stone, Herbert L. and Alfred F. Loomis, *Millions for Defense.* The Derrydale Press, 1934.

Stone, Herbert L., William H. Taylor and William M. Robinson, *The America's Cup Races.* W. W. Norton, 1970.

Strauss, E., *Sir William Petty, Portrait of a Genius.* The Free Press, 1954.

Thompson, Winfield, *The Yacht America.* Charles E. Lauriat, 1925.

Thompson, Winfield M. and Thomas W. Lawson, *The Lawson History of the America's Cup.* Privately published, 1902.

Trease, Geoffrey, *Samuel Pepys and His World.* Charles Scribner's Sons, 1972.

Turnbull, Archibald Douglas, *John Stevens: An American Record.* Century, 1928.

Vanderbilt, Harold S.:

Enterprise: The Story of the Defense of the America's Cup in 1930. Charles Scribner's Sons, 1931.

On the Wind's Highway: Ranger, Rainbow and Racing. Charles Scribner's Sons, 1939.

Waugh, Alec, *The Lipton Story: A Centennial Biography.* Doubleday, 1950.

Picture Credits

Index

Printed in U.S.A.